IN THE PALACE OF SERPENTS

IN THE PALACE
OF SERPENTS

An Experience of Peru

TOM POW

CANONGATE

First published in Great Britain in 1992 by
Canongate Press Plc, 14 Frederick Street,
EDINBURGH EH2 2HB

The right of Tom Pow to be identified as the author
of this work has been asserted by him in accordance
with the Copyright Design and Patent Act 1988.

Illustrations copyright © Chad McCail

ISBN 0 86241 362 1 paper

The publishers acknowledge subsidy from the
Scottish Arts Council towards the publication of
this volume

British Library Cataloguing-in-Publication Data.
A catalogue record for this book is available from
the British Library.

Typesetting by Hewer Text, Edinburgh
Printed and bound by Billings, Worcester

for Julie

Acknowledgements

I would like to thank Stephanie Wolfe Murray of Canongate Press for the confidence with which she said, "Write us a book," when I outlined my travel plans to her. She has been a sympathetic and enthusiastic editor.

I also wish to acknowledge the generous contributions of the following people in the final stages of this book: Mike Gonzalez, Francis Corcoran, Jim Forrest, Chris Rose, and Julie who has been with me all the way.

To all those who helped me before and during my trip, my sincere gratitude.

My sun, the golden garden of your hair and *When I come to visit you* are from *Technicians of the Sacred* published by Doubleday and Co.

I'm getting out & going some 30 kilometres towards the coast is from *The Spider Hangs Too Far From The Ground* by Antonio Cisneros published by Jonathan Cape Ltd.

History of Peru and *Rosaura Beneath The Rain* are from *Reunion elegida* by Washington Delgado published by Selgusa Editores; both translated by Tom Pow. *History of Peru* first appeared in *Cencrastus*.

A Call To Certain Academics was translated from the Quechua by William Rowe.

Loving, Writing by Tom Pow was first published in *The Scotsman*.

The extract from *The Ship* is from *Rough Seas* by Tom Pow (Canongate Press)

My thanks to Alastair Reid for allowing me to use his letter to me.

I would like to thank the Scottish Arts Council and Dumfries and Galloway Education Authority for enabling me to make the journey.

Contents

'What kind of country is this where, by just going from one place to another, you turn into a gringo or a Martian?'
The Real Life of Alejandro Mayta Mario Vargas Llosa

But on the other hand . . .

'There is nothing more edifying and pleasant than to bury yourself in the society of people who belong to an entirely different race, whom you respect, with whom you sympathise, of whom you are, however alien, proud.'
Journey to Armenia Osip Mandelstam

Introduction

In 1987 I received the following letter from the Scottish writer Alastair Reid with the address PO Box 104, Samaná, Dom Republic and the date 3 January.

Here it is just plain beautiful. I've turned very rural. We planted the whole hillside in ginger – maybe that's my destiny, to be a ginger farmer – and cut down a lot of coconut palms. Ginger fetches good prices, coconuts next to nothing. And I bought a small boat for fishing – two neighbours are fishermen and they keep us in fish. And I'm just finishing a second little house, with a real writing room on top, and a solar panel, to have light at night! Luxuries. I'm inordinately happy here, mainly working outside, growing things, swimming etc. The radio is our only technology. I think maybe I'm going soft in the head but it feels good. I have a wonderful girl called Leslie – we discovered Samaná together four years ago, and she comes for the four winter months, speaks Spanish etc. but mainly we delight each other endlessly. She's a TV producer in New York otherwise. She makes the place glow; but so, I suspect, does the fact that it costs almost nothing to live here. In a year or two, the place will actually make a profit. My relief lies in that I don't have to write things to make a living, at least as much as before. I might just stop – but then, as you know, there's the thrill . . .

I'm watching some yeast prove in a glass as I write – it's like an atomic explosion, clouds and clouds. This place has given me an eye for small miracles. So I'm off to make bread.

See if you can get a hold of Nicholas Rankin's *Dead Man's Chest* on RLS – endlessly diverting. Forgive my small writing – it's a small writing day. Keep warm.

Alastair

I decided – as who would not? – that given the chance I should like to visit Alastair in paradise. In the first months of 1989 such a possibility presented itself in the form of a Writers' Bursary from the Scottish Arts Council and a sabbatical from my teaching job.

'Great! Come for February,' Alastair suggested on the phone from his room at the *New Yorker* where he has been a staff writer for many years.

'Alastair, tell me, is Peru anywhere near the Dominican Republic?' I asked. 'I've always wanted to go to Machu Picchu.' Yes, my journey took shape as haphazardly as that.

'If you're going to visit South America, you really must go to Rio,' one plump travel agent told me.

'You think so?'

'Oh yes. For my money it's the most exciting city in South America.'

'Okay.'

'And La Paz – Bolivia – is very near Machu Picchu. And you could fly from there to . . .'

But I didn't want to fly everywhere so I changed my travel agent to the experts – Journey Latin America. They are staffed in London by a group who collectively seem to have covered every inch of the subcontinent by all manner of transport and still found time to take courses in counselling. I remember one conversation, of many, which went: 'I've been told it's possible to take a boat along the Amazon from Peru into Brazil . . .'

'Yes, that's possible.'

'Well, I mean, what I'm trying to say is . . . does that sound like an interesting thing to do?'

The moment's silence was more eloquent than the answer.

Even once the planning stage had passed there was an unreality about my trip. For one thing autumn was taken up with a visit to the USSR as a guest of the Soviet Writers' Union. The first great crack-ups of the state ice-cap, not to mention the great cock-ups of the organisation to which my fellow writer Ron Butlin and I were subjected, absorbed me, yet seemed the complete antithesis to the rhythms of the South American continent to which I should now surely be paying attention. Well, I was making preparations, though some of these felt bizarre in a small town in Scotland at the onset of winter.

'I'd like some mosquito repellent, please,' I asked the nice lady in Boots.

'For midges?'

'Mosquitos really.'

'Well, this one here's what the foresters all use. What do you need it for?'

'The Amazon.'

'The oh . . . the Am . . . well . . .' she trilled. 'And are you really . . .?'

Yes, I told myself, I was. Though I seemed unable to get past the health information section squatting like a terrible Hydra at the opening of the *South American Handbook*. 'Listen to this,' I would say to casual visitors who had enquired when I was for the off:

> *Snakebite*. If you are unlucky enough to be bitten by a venomous snake, spider, scorpion or sea-creature, try (within limits) to catch the animal for identification . . .
>
> *Spiders and scorpions*. Precaution: keep beds away from the walls, and look inside shoes in morning . . .
>
> *Dengue fever* . . . No treatment: you must just avoid mosquito bites . . .
>
> *Other Afflictions*. Remember that rabies is endemic throughout Latin America so avoid dogs that are behaving strangely, and cover your toes at night to foil the vampire bats, which also carry the disease . . .

There were pages of this . . .

Between the poles of Alastair's letter and this health nightmare, my imagination swung. So, as I hope I have made clear, this book is about what happened to someone who began his travels largely in ignorance, and the sense he, in the end, felt compelled to attempt to make out of his experiences, not with recourse to libraries on his return but using what was available to him on the spot. It's what we all do, after all. When I flew into the Dominican Republic from New York at the start of February 1989, I was the man who came from near Lockerbie or, as the locals knew it: 'the place where people fell from the sky like rain'.

Caribbean Prologue

The tropical storm began with a pleasant coolness on the side of my face and bare arms. A swirling breeze turned the pages of an open book. The sea was dark, with a horizon that was being lifted into the sky like a metal bar. As the water approached the shoreline it banked up into great white waves which crashed apart on the rocky promontory.

The first spots of rain were a scattering of coins on the patio. We heard them fall dully on the large palm and plantain leaves. When the first rain started there was never long to grab books and papers from the table and to scramble for the dry safety of the house before sheets of rain blew across the living area in a gusty anger and the rain settled into a screen of water. Sometimes it only lasted a couple of minutes – a spectacular wet-show, memory of which the sun would expunge in another two – but this was different. This was La Ponge's rain machine full to the brim and it would be some hours before it rained itself out.

'Leave the plates! Come on!' Alastair shouted above the skirl of wind and rain. The three of us dived for shelter, and soon were calmly anchored round Alastair's mahogany writing desk, playing cards – pinochle – in the lamplight.

The whitewashed room was pleasantly spartan. A boxed-in section functioned both as a clothes store and a raised bed. Books stretched halfway along two walls – 'the Samaná Library' with titles on waves, stars, plants, how things work, how language works; then *Friday* by Michel Tournier, *The Notebooks of Robinson Crusoe* by Iain Crichton Smith, *R.L.S. in the South Seas* by Alanna Knight; the works of Neruda, Borges and Reid. Where the books ended there was a small round mirror and a straw hat. No photographs. No mementos. In crooks and crannies where wooden spars crossed there was Alastair's collection of 'wee things': neat black torches, a shiny new monocular, a compass. It was, for want of a better description, shipshape: the legacy of Alastair's years in the navy during the Second World War. 'The navy taught me to do with very few possessions – to be portable.'

It was cosy sitting hunched round the shining table, leaning back every so often as a kamikaze moth headed for the lamplight. We watched the rainwater trickle in small rivulets under the door, and find a pathway between the cobblestones. This was some storm.

A speargun rested against the wall, close to the door – a reminder that the rain was not alone in driving us inside. Each evening since our nearest neighbours had been violently robbed, when darkness had fallen we had taken our plastic mugs of tea and come inside, looking up from our cards at each small, unidentified sound.

'A gun?' Leslie had said at Rubio's suggestion. 'Get a gun and they'll just come for your gun.'

'Right,' Alastair had agreed. So one afternoon, loyal Rubio – who had told Alastair that he would kill for him if Alastair wished it – had shown Leslie and me what to do with the speargun. He held it at arm's length, his arm shaking with the weight, and from ten feet away fired it into a palm's trunk. I had a vision of it piercing someone's thigh and hauling them in and knew I would not use it. But it stood there in the shadows as a testament to the tension which had escalated quickly since Alastair's visit to the governor in a role which gave him much amusement, that of one of the wise old men.

Apparently the governor's hall had been full of schoolteachers when Alastair had told of the unsavoury events in Puntabalandras. Inaction over a growing number of corrosive thefts had led to this violent robbery. It was now, he said, a straight choice for the people of Samaná between 'turismo o tigreache'. (Tourism or an untranslatable blend of lawlessness with an edge of youthful machismo.) The governor had immediately seized on this as a battle cry – or an election slogan – and risen to his feet, declaiming, 'Yes, that's the choice. Do we want turismo o tigreache?'

Two police chiefs had been summoned, castigated for inaction and results demanded from them. Alastair then, in his most formal Spanish, had told the governor that the humble community of Puntabalandras would be most honoured if the governor should visit it: such a visit would boost morale no end. The governor replied that he would be delighted to make such a visit, but neither he, nor it transpired any of his police force, had transport.

The results of the governor's demands were immediate. The next day, we heard that Aniano's son, a ne'er-do-well known in

the village, uncharitably, as Superfeo – Superugly – had been
arrested, beaten and had talked. His confession had led to the
arrest of Kenko, someone who had once worked for Alastair but
never won his trust. We heard through the village grapevine that
Kenko had been so badly beaten he could not stand. Rubio told us
how they do it. First they hang the prisoner by his ankles, then beat
his lower back and buttocks till his kidneys start to swell. They leave
them to swell. Then the real beating begins.

Kenko could not stand; could not eat. Kenko was dead. Each
time 'the speak' of the village touched us we exchanged wide-eyed
glances; our unease not in words but in long, nodding exhalations
of breath as if we had been winded. When you demanded action
here, it seemed this is what you got. The last rumour, though,
had been premature, for we learned that Theo, the bullish Swiss
ex sea-captain who with his wife Ursula had been the victim of the
robbery, had to go to identify Kenko the following day.

'I just know it was him,' Theo told us afterwards. 'You know, you
can smell it. The height, the voice – everything. Oh, it was him all
right.' When Kenko had been brought before Theo, the wrist-bones
were showing through the flesh. He had stood hunched over in a
corner. Theo couldn't see him properly: the baton was driven into
his stomach. Theo couldn't hear him properly: the baton again.
'I should have had some stones, you know,' commented Theo,
referring to the fact that his assailants had carried out the robbery
with stones and machetes, 'some stones to throw in his face. To
see how he'd like it.'

'But wasn't he masked during the robbery?' asked Leslie,
admirably masking her own distaste.

'Yes, but you know it was him. You don't forget it, something like
that.' Theo spoke with the smugness of authoritative experience.
'And anyway, if it wasn't, he's still one of the bad ones. Let him
burn!'

'I don't know,' Leslie said between deals, 'perhaps I should tell
my parents not to come.'

'Yes,' Alastair nodded, 'it wouldn't be fair to ask them down to a
situation as tense as this.'

'We could always tell them what the situation was.'

'Then they'd just be worried sick about you and wonder what
I'm doing letting you stay here.' Alastair worried himself. Though

she was a slight figure with bobbed blonde hair and bright, blue, Californian eyes, Alastair was convinced that if there was any trouble Leslie would be the one more likely to fight. From a family of four daughters she had learnt early a sense of self-worth that had nothing to do with gender. 'Dad went to the hardware store, I went with him. He was mending the car, I helped him. I never had any sense of inferiority about being a woman.' The 'fight' she had in her came out in her war with the hens that were constantly invading the garden and in the plosive way she spoke Spanish when angry: her elbows pulling her shoulders back, her bottom lip a thrusting pout. Pity the young buck she got in her sights, I liked to think – if this was a fiction and the young tigers not adult islanders with muscular bodies and precious few options, desperadoes who had quelled the bulk of Theo.

'But I wonder why they went for Theo and not us,' said Leslie. The topic of the robbery was endlessly compelling.

'Because Theo's so careless about letting his workers know about money. He pays them wages on the spot; whereas they know I don't keep any money here.' Alastair had found it was a mark of prudence as well as respect to consider deeply one's role and one's behaviour in a Third World environment. He had evolved an etiquette that involved being circumspect with cash and with goods the locals did not have. It is after all both patronising and enticing to 'let them have a shot of the binoculars'. Theo, building in Samaná because it was beautiful and cheap, had minus sensitivity in such matters and paid the price in every way.

'Of course,' Leslie continued, 'that's assuming it's all a local set-up.'

'Yes, it is. If it becomes just a general rob-the-tourists, it'll be different. That's what I hate about tourism – it completely changes relationships in the community. My fear is that you build up good relationships with the community on a personal level. Tourism starts and you're all bracketed together as wealthy incomers.'

'Us and Theo together.'

'Exactly. No allowances made.'

An unfortunate moth had fallen into the globe of the paraffin lamp. Lying on its back by the wick, its legs twitched then stilled.

'Maybe it's time to leave here then . . .' Alastair's comment rippled out into the darkness.

'And do what?' Leslie asked.

'Go somewhere else. I mean the coast here is nice, but perhaps its time has passed. We could go inland. Start again.' Alastair looked down and played with his nails. I could feel his delight in the possibility of new starts, fresh selves – of scaffolding collapsing and a boat, new-named, being launched into an open sea. 'Sailing is such fun!' Robert Louis Stevenson had written. But for the moment, when he looked up and his blue-chip eyes were smiling, it was obviously just an idea he could enjoy: his playfulness, a little devilment that knew it would not get past Leslie's determination not to be intimidated.

'No, I don't think it would be right to leave now. We've invested a lot of time and effort getting into this community and the relationships I've built up with the people here are valuable to me. I wouldn't feel right just lifting and running at the first sign of discomfort.'

Alastair nodded in accord. He was like someone who had just nipped out for a breath of fresh air on a bracingly cold day: invigorated, but glad to be back inside. For a while.

I sat and listened, played my pinochle and put in my tuppence worth. For me, this narrative with which we had become necessarily obsessed was still one being carried out by others. It touched me like a fiction, though the speargun and walkie-talkie I had slept with were real enough. Yet I felt comfortable in this dim glow, sheltering under Alastair and Leslie's experience of the community, their mastery of the Spanish language and South American ways. 'How serious is all this?' I had even asked Alastair. 'Oh, pretty serious,' had been the reply.

Nevertheless, the tightness in my chest had little to do with present dangers but with the fact that my own narrative awaited me. In a couple of days' time I would fly from Santo Domingo, the first American city, to the American subcontinent. What Iain Crichton Smith's Robinson Crusoe had called 'the vast cinema of sensation' awaited me there.

For some time now I had been casually dropping in questions about South America to Alastair and Leslie, questions that had become more finely focused and more anxious as the time of departure approached. 'One thing at a time,' Leslie advised, 'that's what I kept telling myself: deal with the airport, arrange a taxi, fix a hotel room . . .'

But no matter how I tried to reason with all the mental sharks the *South American Handbook* presented me with, no matter how much I enlisted Alastair and Leslie's support, still I felt my open boat was a rickety, vulnerable affair, circled by triangular fins . . .

PART ONE

The best of times,
the worst of times

An Explorer is Born
LIMA

There was a small ad on the notice-board of the South American Explorers Club in Lima that interested me. Petra was looking for people to accompany her on a trip to Cajamarca in the north of Peru, overland to the Marañón River and then up to Iquitos on the Amazon. I took down the phone number and later, when I called, Petra told me in a clear but heavily Germanic accent, 'This is a serious trip, you know.'

'What, no smiling?'

'Yes, but in its place.'

She turned down my invitation to chat about it at the Café Haiti, a spacious, light café on the Plaza de Armas, preferring to meet me at the Explorers Club itself, 'where I have all my maps and can show you my plans'. That was fine by me: I liked the gung-ho atmosphere of the club, the let's-do-it-now attitude; the walls covered with maps, hiking gear, information on jungle trips, river trips, shooting white water: Latin America as a kind of sub-tropical Cresta run.

'If the SA Handbook is the "bible", then the SA Explorers Club is the "church",' their advert proclaimed. And since yesterday I had acquired a buoyant taste for adventure. It was no thanks to the advice for tourists they had dished out that morning at the British Embassy, snug on the twelfth floor of its office block in central Lima. Scanning 'Peru: Travellers' Security', it was difficult to see, as those at Explorers would sneer, where one could safely go outside Lima.

British travellers are advised that there is a serious terrorist problem in Peru, both political and narcotics-related (according to a recent statement by the Prime Minister, 14,000 people have lost their lives since 1980 as a result of terrorism), and that theft from tourists is commonplace . . .

There are two main terrorist groups operating in Peru: Sendero Luminoso (Shining Path) and the Tupac Amaru Revolutionary

Movement (MRTA). The former's aim is to overthrow the government, the latter's to destabilise it. The terrorists' principal weapon is the bomb. There is therefore a significant risk of accidental injury to bystanders. Sendero Luminoso operates mainly in the rural areas whilst MRTA is chiefly an urban guerrilla group. Against this background, an obvious precaution for British travellers is to plan their journeys so as to avoid those areas designated by the Peruvian government as Emergency Zones. These are as follows:

All provinces in the Departments of Junin, San Martin, Huancavelica, Pasco, Ayacucho, Huanuco and Apurimac . . . The Province of Lima in Lima Department and Callao are also subject to Emergency Regulations . . .

Paul Martinez, second secretary and press officer of the embassy, was obviously no disinterested observer of the woes of Peru. His face, boyish with its round glasses, was edged with sadness as his hand roamed the wall-map and in a cracked voice he explained Sendero's plan to encircle the cities from the countryside; to kill them off by creating a vacuum around them. This was the Shining Path to Communism.

'Yes, many of these areas are stunningly beautiful – Huaraz, Ayacucho. I've had a four-wheel drive just sitting in my garage for months. Can't drive it anywhere. A great shame. A great shame.'

'Mmm,' I nodded sympathetically, feeling slightly out of my depth.

'But then your greatest danger is probably getting robbed.' That came as a faint relief after the graphic possibilities of getting blown up or shot. Still, when someone says to me, 'You can't go here; here they kill gringo tourists,' they only have to say it once. Such pragmatism was not for the gringo who was shown in next.

I stood back to accommodate a girl no more than five feet two in height with short blonde hair, wearing grey Rohans, spanking new trainers, a pink blouse and carrying a roly-poly carpet-bag. She did not look more than twenty-two.

'I'm going to go to the source of the Marañón,' she told Paul Martinez matter-of-factly, stretching a finger to the map, 'follow it up here to the Amazon, then up the Napo' – at this point her heels left the floor – 'to live with Indians for a month, then along to the mouth of the Amazon.'

'How?' Paul asked.

'By walking, canoe, donkey.'

I was impressed.

'Well, this area's very dangerous – narco-traffickers, terrorists.'

'Yes, but I don't think they'll be interested in me. I'm just a tourist.'

'Well, our advice would be . . .'

'I've got all sorts of letters of recommendation. You see, I'm a travel writer.'

Sitting in a dark café later, Natascha told me that that had been the hardest thing to say. Starving, she had ordered a cheese sandwich and a beer but had been unable to finish either.

'I usually live on cornflakes,' she giggled. It did not sound like explorers' fare.

'Have you done anything like this before?' I asked.

'No. I wrote some of the *Rough Guide to Germany* but that doesn't count. I'd always just wanted to go up the Amazon. I wrote to a few publishers and was amazed when one wrote back offering £500 advance.'

'What do you know about donkeys?'

'Just what you learn at the seaside,' she laughed.

'Ever been canoeing?'

'No. And before you ask, the highest I've ever been is the GPO Tower in London and I felt sick.' Her blue eyes sparkled with the happy knowledge that nothing anyone could say to her would put her off: and, outside the Explorers Club, all the prognosis came down on the side of robbery, rape and murder. But as the light caught the shell of her ear I noticed a seam of tiny holes: in her own way Natascha was desperately serious and prepared, and earrings were no advantage on the Amazon.

I left the dusty drag of Avenida Arica and found my way back to the scarred door of Avenida Republica de Portugal 146. Like many doors in Lima it was edged with steel and had no give when I hammered on it. I waited in the humid heat of mid-afternoon, just one more of the legion of steely adventurers come to do battle with the failing infrastructures of this continent to realise a dream. The door clicked open and, two at a time, I took the stairs up to the main room of the South American Explorers Club.

Petra was writing someone a note when I materialised. She would be with me in a minute.

She was blonde – short, utilitarian blonde – with no surplus flesh at all. Her trousers and T-shirt fitted snugly and she had breasts like saucers. Coolly appraising my possible companion I noted the fair down on her arms and along the clean line of her jawbone. Her hands were square, practical; her handshake firm. From the first moment she looked at me intently with deep blue eyes.

'Tom, come this way.' We passed a dim room where a robust, bearded explorer was poring over a map and entered a small, empty room.

'Sit down' – she indicated a wooden stool – 'and tell me why you are in Peru and what your plans are.'

'Well, I've eh . . . I've always wanted to see Machu Picchu . . .'

She blinked at me and leant forward a little. It seemed my reply had been inadequate.

I felt suddenly envious of Natascha's iron conviction. 'I've just always thought it looks so . . .'

'Come over here and I'll show you my plan. I have been working for a tour company for six years in Peru, organising adventure holidays and this is going to be a fact-finding trip. Look at the map.' I looked. 'We will take the bus – to here. And walk around here. Then walk – to here. And hike around – here. Then take a truck . . .'

Each 'walk around' section was dark brown on the map and surrounded by many tight, narrow lines. But the talk of unexplored areas, of uncontacted Indians made the project sound very appealing. I found myself nodding with someone else's head.

'What will I need? I mean, I've no sleeping-bag.'

'*No sleeping-bag*? Oh, that's vital.'

'And no backpack.'

'*No backpack*! Then, how do you . . .'

I leaned over and mimed lifting my hold-all. This was of heavy canvas with leather trim, a gentleman's weekend bag I had bought in a sale the week before leaving Scotland. I was thrilled with it: I had heard so many stories of rucksacks being slit if they weren't covered with chicken wire (chicken wire wasn't in my Spanish dictionary) and anyway at thirty-eight I felt I was too old to be a backpacker. I had thought my priorities should be somehow, well – different.

However, this tight, much-discussed decision was almost nullified at Lima Airport where I had stood staring at barren rollers with eyes like a panicked rabbit. A stewardess had come running up to me: 'Are you Mr Pow? Ah, you're lucky: your luggage is in Rio.' This was my introduction to South American 'luck'; for during a whole, hot week, my bag was lost in a Bermuda triangle between Rio, Caracas and Lima, with occasional placatory but largely false sightings. On two visits to the Venezuelan airline office to pick up a twenty dollar clothing allowance, I talked up the loss of all my non-existent 'jungle gear' and while the elegant supervisor phoned through the motions, I filled her office with some of the sour smells of decay with which Lima had coated me. Awaiting her sincere apologies, I had breathed deeply and slowly recited to myself Elizabeth Bishop's 'The art of losing isn't hard to master . . .'

I put down the imaginary hold-all.

Petra had me fixed with laser-sharp eyes. 'Have you done much backpacking before, Tom?'

I knew she wasn't referring to all my summers hitching across Europe. And besides, when someone uses your name tagged on like that when there are just the two of you, be assured that person has your number. I felt Petra staring into my innermost, truest self and seeing someone who likes to sit for hours in a café, say Café Haiti, with a notebook and a novel. How could I lie?

'Not really.'

'Well, you see the others have. There is an American naturalist, another tour guide and a Peruvian who climbs a lot. I think it is best for the person if they're to get the most out of the trip to be experienced and fit.'

I am lard before her eyes.

'I think, Tom, it is better for you if you go down to Cuzco, see Machu Picchu, hang around. See Peru. You'll find people who want the kind of holiday you do. Okay?'

An image of such people flashed before me: I found myself attracted to their ease yet repelled by their decadence. 'Yes, you're probably right.'

And so ended the illusion, for me, that when you are away from home you are a different person, capable of doing whatever is imagined. Pow the Explorer, as Borges might have put it, 'is another.' Pow himself had been sussed by a professional. It takes all sorts . . . I need feel no shame . . . Yet I slunk past the gung-ho receptionist and in Avenida Portugal breathed dust and freedom both.

*

I met Natascha and her new friend Abby at Café Haiti the next day. I was late because I had taken the wrong colectivo. (These are the battered dormobiles which drift up and down the main avenues of Lima.) I was coming into town from the suburb of San Isidro where I was staying with a friend of a friend who had tolerated my limited wardrobe while cautioning me not to expect my luggage ever to be seen again.

A sharply dressed Italian in the jewellery business noted my confusion and escorted me through the busy streets. My gratitude towards him was softened by the fact that my disorientation was exaggerating his ease, his colossal, young-buck savoir-faire. I fed him questions for his pleasure.

'Oh yes, it's possible to make a lot of money here. Indeed it's dangerous. You've got to be street-smart. But I was two years in Bogotá in Colombia and I am from Genoa. And besides, some people, you know, they like the danger. It gives them – an edge.'

'You?'

'Yes, I like it. I like it.'

We arrived at a crossing thick with traffic; ahead the Jiron de la Union seethed with its gauntlet of hawkers. Lima seemed to me like a city turned inside out.

'Did you see what I did there?' my guide asked. I felt for my passport strung around my neck.

'No.'

'Took off my watch.'

I nodded my enlightenment enthusiastically and he squinted at me like a cat.

The Plaza de Armas was quiet: heavily armoured policemen parading its perimeters and prowling riot-vans ensured that. Inflation had been running at forty-two per cent the last two months and there was tension and dissatisfaction in the heavy air.

Natascha was wearing a jungle shirt with huge front pockets which made her look even slighter and more gamin-like. She had not had a good day. An army spokesman had told her to abandon her trip. I told her I had asked Petra what she thought about the trip.

'Mad. On her own? Crazy. A donkey with all that expensive equipment. She'll be killed, robbed or raped. I've been working in Peru for six years and I'd never travel alone. Does she speak Spanish?'

'A bit,' I had mumbled.

'Well,' said Natascha, her face not even glimmering with doubt, 'I'm going to do it. I'm determined. I've thought about all the risks and I'm prepared for them. I've prepared myself as well as I can physically and I'm mentally prepared too.'

'Good for you,' chimed Abby, sweeping her hair from her face yet again, leather thongs from her wrists the last to clear it.

'Yes, and I reckon because I'm a woman on my own people will be more likely to take me in and help me.'

'Yeah,' Abby started in a time-warp of sixties positivism, 'paradoxically, it's because you appear so vulnerable that you're safer than if you'd been in a group.'

They nodded together happily.

'Mmmm,' I said.[1]

Since my audience with Petra, I remained blissfully free of any illusions about myself; and my purpose had not wavered. I was using a Scottish Arts Council Writers' Bursary to come to South America to write. 'Writing in interesting places' was my self-chosen theme and in the very halting, immensely frustrating way allowed by Peruvian transport, I edged down the coast from Lima, to Nazca, to Arequipa. From there I travelled across to Juliaca at the head of Lake Titicaca and up to Cuzco, arriving there in mid-March at the end of the rainy season. The journey formed a great hook of over sixteen hundred kilometres, the end point of which was Cuzco, sitting in the Andean highlands three and a half kilometres above sea level. One hundred and twelve kilometres further on was Machu Picchu, my goal.

Peru is a vast country two and a half times the size of France that is geographically (and psychologically) divided into what the Peruvians refer to as 'the three realities': '*costa, selva y cordillera*' (coast, forest and mountains) with their peoples, '*costenos, nativos y serranos*'. The journey to Cuzco took me through two of these terrains and the unacknowledged, silent fourth – the desert. An old geography book I had picked up from the school library had sketched in the three regions while casting a dark shadow across the option of flight.

[1]*An Amazon and a Donkey* by Natascha Scott-Stokes (Century) was published in 1991. Without giving anything away, it is an involving read, though slightly misleading about our meeting: 'I came across a Scottish poet . . . hiding in taxis . . .'

It is no criticism of air services in Peru, to draw attention to three air crashes that occurred there in a matter of a few months in 1955 to illustrate three different physical environments. One aircraft crashed in the tropical forest of the interior of Peru and was never found. Another aircraft crashed into a snowfield on the side of a mountain in the Cordillera Blanca, the scene in 1970 of a disastrous avalanche; the plane has never been reached but can still be seen. A third aircraft crashed in the coastal desert region and was located by rescuers, but they found difficulty reaching it due to the absence of roads in the area.

While the joys of flight awaited me, land travel in Peru I found was best thought of not in terms of distance but of ungainly lumps of time. Generally these were of about ten hours' duration which most significantly never came when you wanted them. 'Don't travel on buses at night,' advised Paul Martinez. 'Many of them are being stopped and the passengers robbed. If you're going to Arequipa, break your journey at Nazca.' Fine. The only problem with that was that the bus from Nazca to Arequipa left at two in the morning. 'You'll be okay when it gets to the Pan-American highway,' comforted someone from a party of three going in the opposite direction.

Still, there was the train journey from Arequipa to Juliaca to look forward to. The *Handbook* painted the picture.

> The early morning scene as the day train from Arequipa winds its way up the valley towards Juliaca is enchanting. Winding around Misti and Chacani the train climbs steadily past Yura, Socosani and Pampa de Arrieros; after another 80 km it reaches Crucero Alto, the highest point on the line (4,500 metres). Lakes Lagunillas and Saracocha are very pretty and both come into sight at the same time from opposite sides of the train, which skirts their margins for nearly an hour . . .

The problem here was that the only train to Juliaca travelled there at dead of night; its only view a grey, dismal dawn.

Undaunted, each day I dutifully filled my journal, worked at poems, a play or translations. I moved at my own pace, staying only in single rooms. I enjoyed a certain feeling of detachment as I noted down both poverty and gringo racism; and also a sensation of pride as my writing grew. In sunny, spartan rooms I placed my shoulder-bag on rickety, wooden tables pulled to my bed and laid out my journal, my poems, my play.

And as I travelled to Cuzco, so I took my first faltering steps through the deep minefield of race in Peru. Avoid the term 'Indio', I was told – seen as an insult. 'Campesinos' were what the native population had become. But a 'campesino' according to my dictionary was a small, peasant farmer. Where then did that leave the urban mass of the poor, the shanty-dwellers, the homeless? To call them 'native Americans', another option, would have seemed to confer on them a dignity that could only be ironic given the reduced circumstances of most of their lives. But whatever the terminology, it was a minefield that grew more dense the longer I traversed it: to 'Indio, campesino, costeño, nativo, serrano' were added 'negro, blanco, mestizo, cholo' . . . When was someone simply a Peruvian?

Though it would take me all my time to make some sense of this complex taxonomy of poverty, geography and blood, I soon learned to see myself not just as a traveller or a sympathetic tourist but with the additional cumbersome identity of a gringo.

Gringos!
ON THE ROAD TO CUZCO

I

There was Hilary, for example, who was undertaking her travelling year with a sheer, single-minded competence. Hilary wore her hair up and had a nose like a compass needle: her opinions in my short experience of her rarely wobbled and in the end always found an unquestioning true. In Nazca she had told me in her magisterial English, clipped, no-possible-interruptions voice, 'The flight over the Lines is supposed to be very unpleasant. I'm only in Nazca to break the journey to Arequipa on the advice of the embassy. Frankly I'm not particularly interested in the Lines. I'd rather look at the postcards and hang on to my thirty-five dollars.'

She had just been in India and summed it up as 'physically gruelling – huge distances and people so interested in you, they wouldn't leave you alone. But it wasn't mentally gruelling like Peru is. I think we'll just do our bits and pieces here – the Colca, Machu Picchu, a bit of walking in Huaraz – and head for Ecuador.' She nodded back to her chubbier, quieter companion, the one who did not want to go to Argentina. ('*Why?* Well, because we've just been at war with them, haven't we?')

At Pension Guzman in Arequipa I found them and some other gringo tourists preparing for the infamous Arequipa to Puno night-ride which the *Handbook* warns is 'worked by professional thieves'.

They were heaving their rucksacks into canvas sacks, cutting slits for the shoulder straps. The atmosphere was of a military operation and the rucksack was a very tight fit, so it was between gasps that Hilary told me, 'Yes, we were going to – do the Colca but – we've got this train ride – hanging over our heads and there's a load of people doing it – tonight – so we're going too.'

I envied Hilary her confidence and her efficiency in tackling the irritants of South American travel and her ability to harness others to

21

her ends. At the same time I felt uneasy about the imperial disinterest she showed for all native populations.

Like Hilary, most of the gringo tourists I met on the way to Machu Picchu carried the ember of a little mounted conquistador still burning in their hearts, though none was ruled by it in such a swaggering, narrow-minded way as Ross, a thickset Australian I bought a ticket for in the crush of Juliaca station, the midway point on the train journey between Arequipa and Cuzco.

'Cheers, mate.' His pack was covered in chicken wire and the daypack on his chest was draped with a chain and padlocks. 'Just got all this shit for Peru. Everywhere else, no problem.'

Where else had he been?

'Argentina, Chile, Brazil.'

How long had he been going?

'A month. Yea, I've been moving pretty quick. Just been having a quick squiff at some places. Going to put on the brakes now, though. But I've seen some good spots. Chile: good spot. Brazil: good spot. Travelled with a friend in a car there. Only way to travel, mate, only way.'

On the packed train from Juliaca to Cuzco a small boy trying to make his way out of the carriage, to steady himself, laid a hand on Ross's shoulder. Ross picked his hand up by the wrist.

'Get your hand off me, you little black cunt.'

I forgot whatever I was saying at that moment and fell backwards into verbal mutterings as Ross proceeded to tell me, yeah, he had been collecting addresses all over the world for this trip.

'Christ, but I won't be going back this way. All these people slobbering over you. And some of them stink.'

I came across Ross again in a street in Cuzco. His broad face was unshaven and puffy. He fingered a cut across his nose and pulled on a cigarette. 'Not feeling too great, mate. Too much . . .' and he bent his drinking elbow by way of explanation. 'Got into a fight. Can't remember a thing about it.'

While we talked in a light drizzle, a Peruvian came up and asked if Ross was ready to come and apologise to the woman whose house he had broken into and for the commotion he had caused there. Ross looked at me sheepishly. 'Yeah, I did go looking for the guy,' he admitted; then added weakly, 'But I felt I never touched him.'

I left Ross being led off, looking drained, confused and empty of any understanding. He never got my address and Hilary would not have been remotely interested in acquiring it. I last met her and her friend in Cuzco also, ordering huge slabs of chocolate cake for breakfast. Two blond, tanned, sinewy New Zealand men were with them and they all glowed with delight. Together they had just done the Inca Trail and Hilary had bagged Machu Picchu.

II

Colin was the polar opposite of Hilary and Ross. He was from Yorkshire; a shambling six feet in a floppy, navy crewneck with blond, moppy hair he was constantly running his hands through. He had an attractive face with intense blue eyes but there was a softness, an indeterminacy about it, only partially explained by his nineteen years. We first met in a café in Arequipa where the size of my ears must have marked me out as a suitable confessor.

'I came over here,' he began, 'to live with a family in the north for three months but I got bored after three weeks and started travelling. In Lima I was involved in an accident coming back from a late-night club in the back of a truck. It happened at a crossroads. I didn't know the driver was drunk. I was thrown clear but knocked unconscious. When I woke up I had a great gash down the back of my head – you can see they had to shave my hair – and I had bruised ribs. I was lucky. So then I thought I'd go back to my original plan to go and live with a Peruvian family and make Peruvian friends. But I got bored again really quickly and I couldn't stand the thought of going home without having seen anything in Peru that anyone's heard of, so I sent for money from my parents and started this. But I've very little money so I've got to watch everything.

'Yes, when it happened I just really wanted to go home. Even now I can't wait for my flight back. I don't know but I just can't relax here. Peruvians always want something from you, don't you find? They're always asking, "How much did that cost?" or telling you what they do and asking how much they'd earn in Britain. Then they say, "Do you think I could get a job in Britain?" And I always say, "I don't know. It depends on your qualifications and experience." And then they say, "If I came to Britain, you'd help me would you, amigo? I could stay with you." And I think, Lord, no. Already I'm in a panic when I think who's got my address. I dread them turning up in ten years' time saying, "Remember me." I don't know, even the people who put me up – I have said I would help their daughter but I really hope I don't have to. It seems to me somehow we're more interesting to them than they are to us.

'I'd just thought I would race down here, see Machu Picchu as quickly as possible and get back to Lima. But once I started travelling, I started to quite enjoy it. I can look at all the distance I've travelled and feel a sense of achievement. It's better moving than hanging around all these places wondering what you're doing there. But now this guy's got me a ticket for the tourist class to Puno. And I wanted to go economy. I wanted the danger, the tension. I mean that's all part of the experience of Peru, isn't it? I wanted to do it the way Paul Theroux and all these guys did it. And now I'm doing it the safe way accompanied by the hotel owner's nephew because he thinks it'll be safer. But, hey, listen, I must give you the names of the two hotels I'm most likely to be staying in in Cuzco.'

Colin: nervous, confused, giving himself report cards all the time or seeking absolution as if Peru were some great test or rite of passage. When we did eventually meet in Cuzco, he was feeling guilty that the best time he had had in Peru had been going to Machu Picchu with a gringo. He was counting the days and the dollars he had left till he got back to Lima and his flight home.

'Oh, I just can't wait,' he sighed.

On a napkin I wrote out his dates and opposite each something to do, ending up telling him, 'Lord, Colin, look, you're running out of time.'

Still, he went to the travel agent to book his train to Puno two days earlier. 'I don't know,' he explained, 'I'll just feel more secure when I'm in Lima.'

I noted as he talked apologetically to the travel agent he twisted his fingers behind his back like a nervous schoolboy in front of a teacher who had some hold over his future.

'I'll go back home, I suppose, and try to start up my life again. If my A-level results are good I'll do something in computing perhaps. I'd quite like to work abroad.'

III

At a little more than halfway on the route between Lima and Cuzco, Arequipa is a pleasant, airy city to spend some time in whether you want to or not. There isn't much of a sense of 'through traffic' in Peru: you've really got to work at making that link! And often to the neophyte the mechanics of merely buying a ticket can seem as complex as a masonic ritual. So there's a good chance that whoever you meet in Arequipa you will run into some time in Cuzco. It worked that way with Hilary, Ross and Colin – and also with Roland and Karlson. Both of them had been travelling on their own for some months and together in Arequipa they emanated some of that instant energy and delight of the recently met in a country where solo travel can be a tense experience.

Roland from Bremen was well over six feet with long blond hair down to his shoulders and what passed for a beard in a beardless land but which as a boy I had known as 'bum fluff'. He wore a leather vest and a heavy black leather coat over his shoulders; but his pride and joy was a brown stetson with a ponytail of real human hair which he'd bought in Ecuador. He cut a striking figure as he loped along and he enjoyed the attention he received, always acknowledging any salute with a chopped, backward wave and a smile. His romantic appearance, however, was not sustained closer than waving distance. A heavy brow and jutting chin gave him a slightly concave face; and he had a habit of tilting his head up, exaggerating the jut and staring with his blue eyes over the top of your head as he spoke – English with just the trace of a German accent: spoke and spoke and spoke. Roland was not a good listener.

'I came down through Central America and none of these countries, Nicaragua, Salvador, are as bad as this one. I mean there's something really wrong with this country. Nothing works as it should. I mean in Germany we have certain ideas that everyone accepts, that there should be a minimum wage, that everyone's entitled to health care. But here . . . I couldn't live in any of these countries. You know, whenever I go to a film here, like *Moonwalker* last night, I wonder what do these people make of it? When they come out what are they thinking? I mean when I see that I think, that's my world, but them, what do they think? You know, one thing I don't like about being here is that I'm the rich one. In America I was the poor one and no one bothered me. But here all the time I am a gringo with money and I don't like it. I don't give to beggars. I don't think it's any solution. It just makes the problem worse. I don't know, at the end of this year maybe I go back to Germany to study – physics and philosophy – or I send for money and travel for another year. I realise one year is not enough for South America.'

Roland. I met him again in the Govinda, a vegetarian Hare Krishna restaurant in Cuzco. He ordered a bowl of soup and, like a character from a Dostoyevsky novel (which would have flattered him), produced two rolls from his vast coat to supplement the meal. Here he had developed his thesis and he carried on even more intensely about what was wrong with Peru and how everyone was a robber; thinking that what he came up with were perceptions, not prejudices viewed through his fiction of a shining Germany where there was no poverty, no immigrant workers, no small tight villages where the fairy tales of Hollywood were as remote as to any Latin.

The happiest I saw him was at Aguas Calientes when he told me he and a Colombian had got into Machu Picchu for nothing, after hacking their way up there through a forest. For him such rigid economies bought time. 'This country, they are all just robbers.'

IV

While I had actually seen Roland staring out a beggar-woman, I could only imagine Karlson ruffling a child's hair; shadow boxing; playing dead. I knew he had that capacity in a different situation. But Karlson had been burned.

He was from Hamburg but there was a rude country health about his stocky frame, short fair hair and open, tanned face. At *Moonwalker* he had whooped with delight when the lights went out, relishing any shared catcalls at Michael Jackson's egocentricities. Leaning back on the rickety wooden seats, he had been expansive and at ease, something of a luxury in Peru. To be with him was to share the pleasurable discharge of his energy; but unlike Roland he did not preclude a response.

However it was a different Karlson I joined in the hotel forecourt at quarter to five one chilly morning. He was going to queue for train tickets to Puno for Roland and himself and I was going for a five fifteen bus to the Colca. We unlocked the heavy outer door and stepped out into the street.

'Oh-oh, shit,' said Karlson.

'What's wrong?'

'Looks dangerous.'

Karlson had been in a bus coming from the north of Peru which was held up above Trujillo. One man made it stop and three others, all armed, boarded. They had not found Karlson's moneybelt before the police arrived. 'It was shooting,' Karlson said, cocking fingers on both hands, trying to tame the experience which had made him understandably nervous and a bit confused about what he wanted to do next. 'I just don't know. I need time. I just want to relax. You know. Just to relax.'

The first hundred yards or so of the road were in half darkness then the pale streetlights began. We walked down the road, Karlson like a gunfighter, peering into doorways and alleys – 'If it was an hour later, the chances would be better' – while I chatted animatedly, trying to ease the tension.

On a street corner a stooping man unlocked the front of a drinks trolley to release a hunched-up, sleeping woman. She would be first on the street, beating every dollar-hawker and shoeshiner.

At the 'bus station' – the street booth in front of which my bus would leave – we waited.

'I'll just wait a little longer with you,' said Karlson, gently exhaling his words. 'It's early yet.'

'You should have done this together,' I said with an image of Roland spread-eagled and silent below his precious hat, waiting for the seven thirty alarm when he would amble down to relieve Karlson.

'I know it. I know it.'

Karlson was in South America to learn Spanish. He was a tour guide in Germany and felt Spanish would be useful to know. He felt learning it in Spain would have been too easy. 'But this! This is one hell of a difficult country. Difficult to trust people here.' And Karlson liked to trust but . . .

'Watch these three,' he said, pointing out three boys with baseball caps and ragged T-shirts. 'We were told about them yesterday. Shit, but these people have nothing. If I was them I'd be a robber too.'

The bus was almost finished loading. I showed Karlson the ticket with my name scrawled on it: 'Tampon'. We shook hands; I thought of Colin and we agreed Peru really was a holiday destination for grown-ups.

I met Karlson once more, striding down from Machu Picchu, red with the sun, smiling in the rain. He told me how, happily, Roland had failed to get up in time to make some connection and he himself had spent some days alone on an island in Lake Titicaca.

'Taquile or Amantani?' I called after him.

'Amantani! You've just got to look where the gringos are going!'

The Twitcher and the Snake
CUZCO

I

The Incas saw Cuzco as 'the navel of the world.' They conceived it in the form of a puma and its heart was the ceremonial site which was now the Plaza de Armas. It was a large open square with low hedges enclosing six small gardens with bush-like trees. The surrounding buildings were two-storeyed, the upper built out and supported by a series of arched cloisters which every evening were thick with alpaca jerseys, rugs, cheap jewellery, bargain hunters and cloying money-changers. Wooden balconies jutted out from the upper storeys, giving the plaza not only a feeling of space but of intimacy.

Three buildings dominated the square. The cathedral was built in the early seventeenth century on the site of the Palace of Viracocha, the Inca's Creator deity. Despite its two huge bell-towers, its baroque façade was more palatial than ecclesiastical. To its left the church of La Compañia de Jesus, built in the late seventeenth century on the site of the Palace of Serpents, had a similarly ornate façade. Overlooking both, as it overlooked the whole valley of Cuzco, were the awesome ramparts of Sacsayhuaman, the teeth of the puma which legend has it cost thirty thousand lives to build.

From the balcony of the Cross Keys – available for rent to tour parties during religious processions – you had a good view of all three. To get there you had to pass an unsteady table of jewellery and climb a flight of worn-lipped, stone steps to the second floor. It felt rather like passing through a magic door in a James Bond movie or slipping into a speak-easy because the Cross Keys was a gringo hang-out par excellence, complete with long, oak-look bar and well-used dartboard. Covering the walls were saddles, bridles, beermats and the personal mythology of its landlord, Barry Walker. These included a photograph of Weisdale Voe, taken from his local in Shetland where he had lived for five years; photographs of himself and friends on Lost City trips; and photographs and posters relating to his prime interests, those of a naturalist, a birder, a twitcher. Like others I would meet, but none more than himself, Barry had found in Peru both challenge and congeniality, even turning its frustrations into occasion for satisfaction. He was particularly proud of his collection of malt whiskies, some bought direct from contrabando. There was free drink for a couple of nights for anyone who arrived at the Cross Keys with a bottle of malt.

'Most of the time I live in the real Peru,' he told me, 'but the Cross Keys is designed to be *Not Peru* – a place where the gringo and the expat who live here all the time can escape from all the hassling, the beggars and all that crap – and relax.'

We relaxed into another large bottle of Cusqueño beer as Barry told me his story. He had qualified at university in geology and geography, had tried teaching in Hull but found it too confining and when one of the old guard told him he should be spending more time with children who had some potential rather than those to whom he felt committed, he resigned on the same day. Then after a year in Israel doing research on migrating birds of prey – 'I've got a great story about that, mate. Remind me to tell you some time over a beer' – he had lived in Shetland for five years working on the rigs.

'There was this other bloke working there. He was a birder too and the pair of us decided to go to Thailand. But there were no flights, so I said, "Look, mate, we're never going to have this amount of money and time again, let's go to the best place in the world for birds – Peru."'

'The best place in the world?'

'Listen, mate, there's something like seventeen hundred species here. In Tambopata Reserve, an area of ten hectares, in the last ten years, there's been more birds spotted than in Great Britain since they began keeping records in 1750. Yeah, about seven hundred birds. In the whole of continental North America, there's only five hundred and fifty. Tell you, mate, if you want amazing statistics Peru's the place.'

Barry was in his early forties, six feet tall and heavily built. He had wide-set brown eyes and a way of gritting his teeth in a half smile, as if against the energy which coursed through him. His thick hair was greying but he had not given up on red baseball shoes, sleeveless T-shirts or what he called his 'cosmopolitan Lancashire accent, half scouse, half Lancashire'. When he was enthusiastic about a subject, and I imagined he would turn his back on anything about which he could not enthuse, he leant forward on his bar stool, his thigh beating against it. Like now, when he was talking about his first involvement with Peru.

'So anyway we flew straight into Iquitos – you could do that then – and spent six weeks going round Peru. We came to Cuzco, went to the rainforest and that was it, I was hooked.

'I still had my job but I couldn't wait to come back here. I came back for a month, met a Peruvian girl and then I got a letter from her giving me a really good reason to come back. I left my croft cottage fully furnished – TV, stereo and all that; two cars as well. Don't know what happened to it all. Never been back.' That was six years ago, and now Barry had two 'really good reasons' to keep him in Cuzco.

'You must be happy here, then?'

'Yes, mate, I wouldn't want to live anywhere else. I've got my ornithology, my Lost City trips – places where no white man's been. Still, the situation's precarious. I mean, the next election if the Right get in they're going to put pressure on the terrorists who in turn are going to hit harder; not great for tourism. Or if the Left get in they're not going to look kindly on gringos catering for tourists. Dodgy situation, mate.' An unusual sight, Barry's face clouding with concern. But it soon vanished when I mentioned my wish to visit Manu National Park.

'Yeah, mate, the trouble with Manu is that there's no cheap way to get there, leastways this time of year. These people at South American Explorers, they don't know what they're talking about. They tell people, "You just get a truck." They don't tell them how infrequently the trucks leave, the red tape you've got to go through.'

I nodded a yeah-they-don't-know-shit nod and something small and mean inside me felt it had got even.

'No,' Barry concluded, 'there's no way to do it for less than six hundred dollars.' He paused briefly to confirm that with Mario Ortiz, a handsome jungle tour guide who tonight was in the early stages of a journey to explore oblivion.

'Tell you what though, mate,' and he was overtaken by another surge of enthusiasm, 'if you're interested, what you could do is take a trip to Explorers Inn in the Tambopata Reserve, see the rainforest there . . .'

'Or wait till I get to Iquitos . . .'

'Listen, mate, if it's pure climax rainforest you want to see, south-east Peru is the place to see it.' Mario nodded sagely.

'Climax rainforest?'

'Hasn't changed since the ice age. Hasn't changed for sixty million years. And you could see an example of ecotourism and also check out Ametra 2001 – it's a centre down there for the study of traditional medicine.' His thigh was beating against the bar stool. 'I'll give you letters of introduction saying you're a writer and to give you any help you need.'

'Would you? That would be fantastic.'

'No problem.'

'I'm excited, Barry, I really am.' I beamed and slugged. Fortuna was smiling on me and my haphazard trip felt as if it was taking some kind of shape, a dynamic and a logic of its own. Likewise Mario's evening when two blonde Australian girls led him uncomplaining away from our company.

'First, though,' Barry said, 'you've got to see Machu Picchu.'

'Dead right. But not before I hear that great story of yours.'

'You want to hear it now? All right, mate, then I really must go. There's a game of darts waiting for me. Here, let's get in another couple of beers first . . .' (It was to be a story with a price. In my excitement I had forgotten all the good advice about acclimatising to altitude and alcohol. The next day I took to the drizzling streets of Cuzco with a hangover of Sacsayhuaman proportions.)

'Cheers, mate. Well, like I was saying I was over in Israel doing research on the migration of birds of prey. You know birds of prey can't fly over water so Israel's part of a kind of funnel for them which makes it a great place to do bird counts. I was paying my own way, sleeping on the beach at night, leaving my backpack in a kibbutz during the day, and the research went pretty well. I wrote a couple of articles about it eventually.

'Anyway I'm a twitcher, one of these mad guys who goes anywhere to see a bird he's not seen before. And I'd seen every bird in Israel but one, the bar-tailed lark. Now the thing with the bar-tailed lark is that it just lives in the desert where nothing else does and to complicate matters it lives in the forbidden zone. Yeah, it makes nothing easy. But when it got to my last week I just thought stuff it, I'm going to give it my best shot.

'I took a bus to the border of the forbidden zone just as close as I dared, got out and saw this nice little wabi, a small valley kind of thing, and thought I'll settle down there and take my chances. Well, then I spotted this encampment of Berbers and thought, God I gotta get outta here . . . But it was too late, their kids had seen me.

'So I'm surrounded by kids, then adults too and dragged down into this tent for tea, and you can't refuse their hospitality, that's really serious business. But they don't speak any English, I don't speak any Arabic, so I'm gesturing away about the bar-tailed lark and not being able to go into the forbidden zone, and somehow or other the leader understands what I'm going on about and makes me understand that because they're nomads they don't have to follow international boundaries. I can sleep in their tent and go into the forbidden zone with them tomorrow.

'Next day this camel drops to its knees and this guy gets on and signals that I've to get on behind him. I clamber on and he puts his great black dress over my head. Now I've never been on a camel before and these guys, I mean, they don't wash; just roll around in the sand. And I'm there bouncing up and down and what with the heat of the sun and the smell – I tell you, mate, it feels like days. But really it's only about three hours. Yeah, long enough.

'Anyway we stop. The camel drops; the guy takes off the sheet and I'm blinded for about two minutes. I get down from the camel and it's nowhere. Really, nowhere. Just dunes. They tell me if I walk in a certain direction for an hour I'll come across a road and by the time I set my watch and compass they've vanished over the dunes.

'Now I'm thinking, *this is it* – the perfect habitat for the bar-tailed lark. Pure moonscape. I've got the binoculars out and I'm about to settle down when over another dune comes this armoured van bombing along, antennae waving like crazy. It screeches to a halt beside me, three guys get out, blindfold me, tie me hand and foot and bundle me into the van.

'We drive for about an hour. I'm pulled out, dragged – manhandled – down a flight of stairs, my blindfold's taken off and my hands freed. I'm in this concrete cell with just a light bulb, nothing else at all, and after the desert it's cold as a freezer.

'Well, I'm left there shivering about two or three hours then I'm taken upstairs and interrogated by these three very heavy-looking military guys. I tell them all about the bar-tailed lark and the Berbers but they're looking at me in a very strange way and I mean now the whole story sounds pretty crazy to me as I'm telling it.

'So I'm taken back down and I'm wondering what the hell's going on. And I'm scared, mate. Now I'm really scared. It's got to me how these guys were looking at me.

'I spend an hour like that – shitting myself – till this guy comes in and says, "We've decided to believe your story. To believe that you have just been incredibly stupid. What we're going to do is take you to the nearest place you can get a bus. You will get a bus to Tel Aviv and we never want to see you again. Never. Understand?"

'So I'm blindfolded again, taken to this bus stop an hour or so away and when that bus comes I'm right on it and no mistake. And that's it. End of story.'

'Amazing story.'

'Yeah, isn't it, mate? But there's a postscript to it. For years I wondered what the hell all the fuss was about. Then seven years later I was reading a newspaper and there was this article about the Israeli journalist who broke the news about the Israelis having nuclear silos in the Negev Desert, and suddenly the coin dropped. That's why they were so paranoid. I was walking around with a camera and binoculars right on top of their nuclear silos. Christ, they could just have topped me. Why should they take the risk?'

'Whew-yow-ee.'

'Exactly.'

'So you never did see the bar-tailed lark?'

'No, mate.' Barry laughed. 'I never did.'

II

Scotland I found to most Peruvians who had heard of the place meant two things: whisky and Cubillas. No, Cubillas was not an exotic mixer but the striker Teofilio Cubillas who, in the world cup in Argentina, pricked the inflated hopes of Ally's Tartan Army with a majestic thirty-yard shot. He was thirty-eight years old at the time – why the hell hadn't we heard of him? He made 'Poor Peru/what Scotland's going/to do to you' probably the most regretted ditty ever penned, as the goal proved to be the most stunning beginning of the end. Peruvian taxi drivers still smiled broadly at the memory.

If this showed their somewhat thin knowledge of my country, the compliment was returned. When I asked the woman in Lima in charge of the government's tourist agency FOPTUR what image of Peru was being promoted to attract a hoped for 780 million dollars worth of tourists within the next couple of years, she told me: 'I could say we have everything here – the three regions, mountains, coast and jungle; beaches and adventure. But the main identity that people know something about is the culture.'

'Meaning?'

'Machu Picchu. Cuzco. The country of the Incas.'

I understood her logic: to anyone, or to be precise to any tourist, who cast an eye towards the subcontinent, Machu Picchu was not only a symbol for Peru but for the whole of Latin America. Certainly the Chilean poet Pablo Neruda saw it that way and his long meditation 'The Heights of Machu Picchu' had ensured that the ancient city acted as a Mecca for all Latin American writers:

> the cradle of lightning and of man
> rocked in a wind of thorns.

Machu Picchu, however, has remained a mystery. Quite who it was built for, how long it was occupied and why it was abandoned are matters for archaeological speculation. It was a different matter with Cuzco, the once imperial Inca city.

There were in fact three different Cuzcos that I could see. The first and most accessible was that used by tourists, rich and shoestring ('poor' was a word with a precise, living meaning here) as a base for their trip to Machu Picchu. When the South American travellers arrived here, they were beginning to feel comfortable within or at least aware of the vast map of the subcontinent. Above them, Ecuador, Colombia, Venezuela; below, the long finger of Chile; to the east, the mammoth contradictions of Brazil edging on to Paraguay and Argentina. In Cuzco they met old acquaintances from Buenos Aires, from Santiago, from Quito. They swopped shorthand descriptions of their routes, their distances. They had tales to tell. And in Cuzco there were bars enough and restaurants enough to tell them in, whether your taste was for pizza, Chinese, French or vegetarian.

Cuzco, however, like Florence, another beautiful red-roofed city, was able to retain its dignity and integrity under the tourist onslaught; to demand that here at least, no matter how flimsy your knowledge, you had to reach some accommodation with the past.

John Hemming's compelling account, *The Conquest of the Incas*, is a brick of a book, not the kind you want to lug around if you can avoid it. I had read it hungrily in Lima when for a time it was the most substantial piece of luggage I possessed. Much of his study of the often shameful encounter between the conquerors and the native Indians was hazy to me now, but the clean lines of the narrative still reverberated within me whenever I saw an Inca ashlar. It told how an empire of six hundred miles wide and nearly three thousand miles long, so big the Incas called it Tahuantinsuyo, the Four Quarters of the Earth, had been engaged in a fratricidal war of succession when its miserable future was planned by two uneducated adventurers, Francisco Pizarro and Diego de Almagro, and by a priest, Father Hernando de Luque. From this time on, from one point of view, it was a dramatic story of courage, endurance and greed, a South American version of *The Good, the Bad and the Ugly* writ large. From another it was simply teased out tragedy which had begun with the cruelly pragmatic strangulation of the Inca (King) Atahualpa in Cajamarca, followed by the systematic looting of the empire's wealth and the suffering of its peoples till the Inca kingdom was reduced to the forest sanctuary of Vilcabamba. But even there they were not to be left alone, and after the last campaign the conquest ended ignominiously as it had begun with the summary execution of Tupac Amaru, thirty-nine years after Atahualpa, his uncle.

The legendary wealth of the Incas sounded almost as unlikely, as marvellous to me as it must have done to Pizarro and his cohorts, many of whom were peasants drawn from an arid future in Estremadura. When Atahualpa offered gold as a ransom for his release Pizarro had asked, 'How much gold?'

'This much,' the Inca reputedly replied, his arm indicating a line as high as he could reach. The room, twenty two feet long by seventeen feet wide, was to be filled once with gold and twice over with silver within two months. Not much of that fabled but very real gold has survived. Most was melted down and shipped back to Spain. Of what has been preserved, much was housed in the Gold Museum in Lima, fortified as Fort Knox. What the gringos left, the gringos today, a drool of tourists, pay five dollars a head to see. Yet the lushness of the case upon case of battered gold left me as cold as the side chapels of Europe with their *trésors de la cathédrale*. I warmed more to the popettes, the fat figures made of rough weave, their big faces improvised from beads, shells and feathers. They seemed strangely modern, suggestively effective as a sculpture by Picasso; they lived in the *now*. In the gold I saw only dead artefacts from some magical past.

The Inca stones in Cuzco also lived in the now. Each one of them. And their preservation was not due to any touristic interest; for in a real as well as a metaphorical sense, colonial Cuzco was built on their foundations as well as on the backs of the native population. On Coricancha, the Inca sun temple, the Spaniards imposed the church of Santo Domingo: yet Coricancha, though long stripped of its golden sheathing, was still Samson – blinded, chained, but with all his dignity intact.

On evening walks down Loreto, a lane of high stone walls, trying to decide on a restaurant, I would stop and run my hands over the ashlars, marvelling at the purity of each one as I have marvelled at the completeness of a sculpture by Brancusi; each of them so tightly locked together that I found it impossible to fit a fingernail between them.

The facilities for travellers and the ever present interest of the Inca remains made this an easy city to spend time in, but the darker side of Peru's history had found its way into the present and thus highlighted the problems of fitting a comfortable tourist face on to a Third World country.

That the economy of Cuzco depended on tourists was not in doubt; but neither was the fact that to those who did not profit directly from them, the tourists were often treated with resentment and distaste: a sneered 'gringo', a refusal to help, a wrong direction given. In such petty ways some revenge was taken on the wealthy transient. After all, exploitation had not stopped with the theft of the gold. A campesinos' strike, which had paralysed Cuzco two weeks before my arrival, had had the rallying cry, '¡Por tierra, paz, precios justos!' For land, peace, fair prices! The volatility of the Cusqueños coupled with the increasing pressure among them of poor campesinos who had come down from the Andes to seek a better life stood in ironic contrast to the rigid panoply of the state; a situation brought home to me on Easter Sunday.

In the packed cathedral I looked past the broad, shining black plaits of the campesinas, the little, pert pigtails of the girls, up the aisle at the scarlet and gold draped Virgin, her arms outstretched in benediction beneath her gold pillared arch. The suffering Christ himself writhed on a green wooden cross on one of the huge side pillars. Catholicism here was a lush affair, its two central images taken to their metaphorical extremes. Easter was a good time to see them.

In Arequipa I had watched women in the church of Santo Domingo giggle happily as they dressed the Virgin for a procession; behaving much as if they had been preparing a girl for a wedding, not a poor girl though, rather one Velasquez might be called upon to paint. While at the other extreme the Christ on the cross was not the Son of God who had made his peace, who had just sighed, 'All is accomplished,' but the still-human man whose body was racked in agony. The Christ-corpse carried in a glass coffin down Plateros, over the design of doves and flowers and cross made out of petals which had engaged so many all day, and borne round the Plaza de Armas, was one whose wounds gaped, who was chalky-white with blood-loss.

Entering the small church at Chivay at the head of the Colca Canyon, children had jumped out of two alcoves and run off laughing. From my hotel window I had watched the tiny procession bearing its little donkey aloft, then seen the children sweep the streets with the palms, startling a piglet from a gutter. Religion there had seemed a natural, relaxed concern. Here in the huge cathedral I was put in mind of all the oppression that had been put in motion with the words, 'You are all God's children.' Christianity was the justification of conquest and exploitation: Atahualpa had died a convert; from the scaffold his nephew Tupac Amaru had denounced the religion of his ancestors as a fraud.

The archbishop and all those in his grand procession were of European extraction; his passing benediction was bestowed like a royal wave. Some time before his entrance, campesinos had rushed and squabbled like geese when another confession box was opened, but now they stood or sat in silence holding their children to them as the liturgy was gone through. It was all very uninvolving, or appeared to be so. I thought again of the awe in which the Indians had come to hold their conquerors. Initially these had been one hundred and seventy-five men and twenty-five horses laying claim to an empire of fourteen million. But once their god-king had renounced his authority, their conversion had been easily achieved.

Then, drifting into the sombre silences, I heard the insistent, unimaginative but slightly humorous ta-ra thump-thump brass and

drums of a military band. I squeezed my way out to find at the foot
of the cathedral steps the white helmets of a military band celebrating
Easter state-style, surrounded by the boy soldiers of Peru in grey,
black and khaki, armed with machine-guns. A commando unit,
wearing black jerseys, gloves and skull-caps, armed with bazookas,
marched past. Always there was a machine-gun turned towards the
crowd.

Still suffering occasional wooziness from the altitude, I sat on the
steps, turned my face to the warm sun and was subjected to my
first unsuccessful robbery: two little nicks in the zip pocket of my
top. I felt nothing at the time and naïvely smiled to myself when I
spotted it later. Perhaps the razor was in action as the dignitaries
were raising the many-coloured flag of Cuzco and the Cuzco song
was being thumped out:

> Cuzco, Cuzco es tu nombre sagrado
> como el sol del Incario inmortal
> todo el mundo te lleva en el pecho
> como canto y bandera triunfal.

(Cuzco, Cuzco is your sacred name/ like the sun of the immortal
Inca river/ all the world carries you off in its breast/ like a song
and a triumphal flag.)

In every city that Easter Sunday, I was told there would be
sermons on patriotism (¡Viva el Peru!); national and civic pride
would be celebrated. Church and state would work together, as they
always had done, in an attempt to create a coherent image of Peru.
It was a fiction that was becoming threadbare in the spring months
of 1989. At Lima bus station an unemployed mining engineer, who
would later sting me for a few thousand intis, told me, 'This country,
something really wrong with it. The man running it, he doesn't know
what he's doing. I think he's a fool.' Suddenly loud music had blared
over the Tannoy. 'National anthem,' he had explained. 'They play
it every day at twelve. Two years ago they play it, everybody stands
up. Now look at them.' Everyone sat slumped beside their bundles,
the sellers moving unconcerned among them.

And in the Plaza de Armas in Cuzco the hollow brass could not
exorcise the ghosts. Here Tupac Amaru had been beheaded and his
spiritual successor, the self-styled José Gabriel Tupac Amaru the
Second, renegade leader of an attempt to restore the pride of the
Incas, was himself executed in 1781. Accounts of the dispatch of

this, the last descendant of the royal line, showed that the cruelty of the conquest did not dim.

First Tupac Amaru had to watch the torture of his son and uncle and other associates before his wife's tongue was cut out and she was slowly garrotted. Then he himself had his tongue cut out, a rope attached to each limb and four horses tried to rip him apart. This they failed to do and to end the sorry spectacle an order came that the executioner should cut his head off. One eye-witness account noted: 'At twelve noon, when the horses were pulling the Indian, there came a great gust of wind, and after this a rain shower which made everyone, including the soldiers, run for cover at great speed. This is the reason Indians have begun to say that the sky and elements felt the death of the Inca that the Spaniards, inhuman and impious, were killing with such cruelty.'

The history of Peru since the conquest consists of such cruelty, contradiction and tragedy: a situation fully acknowledged by the poet Washington Delgado, himself born in Cuzco.

There is no past
without a multitude
of deaths.

There are no Incas, viceroys
or grand captains
without a hundred
yellowing pieces of paper
and a little earth.

A master there was who said
to his slaves: gold is good
and God is in the sky.

A soldier there was who said
to whoever would listen:
I kill because they pay me to;
I don't know what sky is.

But there is no history
without twenty words
that say nothing.

The grandeur of history and the pathos of history were inescapable in Peru. As I noted earlier, La Compañia de Jesus from where Tupac Amaru the Second's messy execution was orchestrated, was built on the Palace of the Serpents. Historical metaphors can never do justice to the complexity of a country's past, but at this early stage of my trip I felt I was beginning to discern a snake's energy and inertia in Peru's past. However, in the tourist centre of Cuzco I could take my knowledge of its markings, no further. I wanted to meet Peruvians and speak to them one to one; and in Cuzco I encountered only the persistence of hawkers, the sullen attention of displaced campesinos, a world that turned itself or me into shadows.

I knew there was another Peru. I had seen it when I had taken a detour from Arequipa into the Colca, reputedly twice as deep as the Grand Canyon. Images from that trip still excited me as I contemplated my journey into the Sacred Valley and to Machu Picchu.

A CONDOR IN THE INCA'S GRAIN STORE

The road winds up the mountainside towards El Misti. Small cairns mark sections where landslides and floods have eaten out great half moons. At times the road is little better than a forestry track. We approach a tight bend: the driver talks to the conductor; the morning sun shines blindingly – I peer over into pure space.

A flat tyre once we've cleared El Misti. All males disembark. El Misti is Fujiyama, its blown-off table-top covered in snow. Men and boys send it arching, watery tributes.

Up on the plain the driver appears to move arbitrarily between barely visible tracks. This is rockscape, moonscape. And those who wait to get on, singly or in groups, where have they come from? Bearing what? The lone cyclist, the donkey rider heading for a distant horizon: wherever they are going the eye cannot follow.

We startle: llamas, their ears tagged with red wool, like haughty sheep; their even more effete sisters, the caramel-coated vicunas; and quivers of buff-backed sierra finches, skimming the pampas like concentrations of energy and light.

Giant cloud shadows cross the vast open spaces of Peru's interior. On the altiplano before the drop into Chivay the height is 4,800 metres, higher than Cuzco or Lake Titicaca. An Englishman whose bus broke down there told me he thought he was dying.

Hours on, a patch of green deep in a valley: and the valley opening on to a maze of broken fields. Herdboys with twigs and day-bundles.

A cross-bar. A sign: 'Peru – land of amazing landscapes'. Five hundred intis, a pittance for the gringo.

At Chivay, a small market town, the bus fills. Sardines. Good-humouredly, bundles are pushed out of the way; babies and children accommodated. Many have stood uncomplainingly for hours. A small boy pulls out a piece of bread, rips off a chew and puts the bread safely back in his pocket.

Women with stiff-brimmed panama hats turned up at the side and pinned with giant rosettes. Thick billowing dresses; blouses embroidered with birds and fish. I watch one sitting on her haunches by her bundle. Like a subject of one of Edward S. Curtis's sepia photographs, her face is wrinkled but beautiful. A stoical metronome, she moves only to brush a hand across her brow from time to time.

At a small village, a hamlet of stone cottages, two boys with loose felt hats and sandals, like ragged street urchins. (Words to take you through time.) One picks up a piece of donkey shit and throws it at his friend who runs off laughing. A teenage girl gets on the bus, then, as if she's just remembered, takes out a comic story magazine and holds it out of the window. The boy's face lights up. He reaches up for it and takes it in both hands. He holds it away from himself as if it is a mirror, or something equally precious. As he walks away, his friend comes up still in a playful mood. The boy with the comic brushes him away and walks off, captivated.

Cruz del Condor. A condor in the Inca's grain store.

Some people are lucky enough to see the condors within ten feet here; to hear the wind riffling through their feathers.

Later a Canadian will tell me: 'It was the worst bus journey of my life and when we get to the Cruz del Condor, people start saying, "Go on then, aren't you going to get out? This is what you've come all this way for." And I think no. If I've got to fight my way back to my seat again, I'll punch someone. So I say to this German girl, 'Here, you take the camera. You get the picture.'

Cabanaconda. Mud and straw-brick houses. Tin or thatch roofs. Muddy lanes with runnels for effluent. Pigs. Dogs. Hardy's Wessex must have looked something like this.

In an earthen-floor restaurant a young girl reaches up to the hatch to bring bowls of strongly coriander-flavoured potato soup to a rickety trestle table.

> 'But you must
> write a poem
> about the condor.'
>
> Though I, as they,
> had only seen it
> from the road.
>
> It must have been
> a lucky stretch
> on the rocky track
>
> that wound high
> above the canyon;
> for the bus held
>
> to the condor,
> as it held
> to the currents
>
> which rose up
> from the valley floor,
> past the terraced
>
> hills to the snow-
> capped peaks beyond.
> It held its wings
>
> like two huge
> black flags – only
> the great pinions

fluttered slightly.
Then it was gone
and we were left,

craning back
into a landscape
that shimmered

with new life.
One minute? Not more.
But there are some

moments one must
make the most of.
From time

to time, everyone
understands this
unpopular art.

At the head of the Colca Canyon behind Cabanaconda, I gaze down at the snaking brown river, at crazy paths that fall through the smoky green evening light. A group of five boys canter up, led by one wearing a stetson. A latecomer hides behind a boulder. They wear torn crew-neck jerseys and, apart from the leader, felt hats over shorn hair. They all have rough red patches like coins on their cheeks, small, tough-skinned hands, and feet encrusted with mud. The leader speaks with an exaggerated wisdom – He Who Knows. He names the valley for me, first in his native Quechua then in Spanish. He points to a distant waterfall like a zag of lightning on the hillside. He's been there. And the city? Sure, he's been to Arequipa (two hundred kilometres away). It's all right but he prefers Cabanaconda. They all nod. They demonstrate how they use their catapults for birds; stage a frightening scuffle at the edge of the canyon, then pose for a photograph with great, old-fashioned dignity.

The bus back to Chivay is at four fifteen a.m. No one complains or even yawns. The driver honks and honks at each stop; peers into the distance, giving the latest comer a chance. Girls, women and small children lug great sacks along to a spot where they can be heaved on to the roof of the bus. What they cannot lift they put between their legs and waddle with to the edge of the bus.

In the covered market at Chivay, the cold dawn lifted, lines of people at trestle tables breakfast on huge plates of spaghetti, rice, potatoes and thick soup, served by women out of steaming tureens. Men lift their ponchos over one shoulder to give themselves a free arm. I buy two ripe mangoes. I show dollars and a five pound note. La Reina Elizabeth. 'Ah.' A group of women gathers, pointing. 'La Reina Elizabeth.'

A walk to the hot springs. The sun just burnishing the barley seas. Stone dykes with mud and cactus on top. A view of the snow-capped peaks of Hualca-Hualca and Ampato through sprays of golden marigolds. The brown river flowing through the embryonic gorge, one side still soft and green, the other barren but starred with cactus like stiff fingers.

I am following two women, heavy bundles on their backs. Their long skirts make them look as though they glide on wheels along the riverside track; both of them hold a spindle, working and talking all their way.

To paraphrase Paul Eluard: There is another Peru, but it is in this one.

Bird-sound. No traffic. No hawkers. No dolares. No comprame, señor, por favor. The dignity of the country. An etiquette. Even the old women manage a slow Bue-nas, just as they're passing you.

The peace of a west coast Scottish island.

In a small restaurant for fresh trout. *EuroHits* is on the TV. The girl asks me what the woman is singing about. I tell her she is singing, 'I am your woman and you are my man. Together we have the power of love.' She stares at me uncomprehendingly.

On the wall is an advert for Arequipeña, the local beer. A blonde Eurasian manages to turn scantily clothed buttock and breast to camera at the same time. Outside, a camera-strapped tourist haggles before he hands over some notes for a photograph of a mother lost in a dome of ragged blankets and the two children who peep out behind her.

'My Sun, The Golden Garden of Your Hair'
CUZCO TO OLLANTAYTAMBO

Like all Peruvian buses the one to Pisac, thirty-two kilometres from Cuzco, was packed. But having arrived in the chill early morning at the point of departure, I had secured a back seat pressed hard against the thin, vibrating metal. I had left most of my gear with the patron at Hostal America, gripping his elbow as I pointed to the shoulder-bag: '*Muy* preciosa, señor. *Muy* preciosa.' He had shaken his bunch of keys at me with great seriousness.

I clutched my daysack on my lap as I watched the clipboard make its way round. On every journey each passenger had to fill in name, age and profession. Something to do with control of terrorism I surmised, but rather a pointless exercise given the haphazard nature of public transport in Peru. I noted the young man beside me now resting the clipboard on his briefcase was Alejandro, a teacher of Spanish. It was an easy entry into conversation and, after going through the statistics dear to a teacher's heart (hours per week – twenty-five: pupils in a class – thirty), I asked him about the problems of teaching Spanish here.

'It's difficult,' he began, 'because the language and the culture is Quechua; but Castellano is imposed on them.' I knew that Quechua, the lineal descendant of the Inca language, was spoken by the majority of the Peruvian Indians and told him that in the Gaelic-speaking parts of Scotland there were similar tensions. There, Gaelic had always been the language of the playground; English that of the schoolroom. Now, ominously, that situation had reversed. Television. He nodded a kind, concerned face that relaxed into a shy smile; he too was enjoying our cultural connection. I asked him the differences between the Quechua and the Spanish view of the world.

'Total,' he asserted. 'The Quechua believes in magic, in the trees, in the sun. There is more sense of community. It's Christian yes,

45

but also . . . Quechua.' I smiled understanding and held on to the last wedge of the broken window, catching glimpses of the brown Yucay River snaking its way between the terraced hills.

'And you,' I asked, hungry to question a culture I had only been able to observe, 'what do you consider yourself to be?'

'¿Yo? Quechua y Peruano. More Quechua but Peruvian also.'

'And what is it to be a Peruvian?'

'To be a mix of the two. A mestizo, which is what I am' – light, coppery skin and regular features – 'is a biological result of the conquest. Culturally I must acknowledge my Spanish blood, but my sympathies are for the Quechua experience. You see historically the campesino has been most exploited. The whole colonial system was set up to exploit and so it continues. Most campesinos live between two thousand and four thousand metres up in the mountains, in the harshest land, and still they are exploited. It's such things that get to your heart.' A slight man, he held himself erect and drew up his portfolio across his chest.

'Then do you feel a little bit Inca?'

'¡Seguro! Of course!' And he smiled broadly.

The climb to the ruined fortress of Pisac above the red-roofed town soon left me breathless. As I panted in the thin air, a herdboy passed me on the broken steps which zigzagged up the mountainside, joining the smooth terraces with their retaining walls of stone. He moved like a ghost, his large upper body rigid, his short legs exact metronomes: evolutionary perfection. As my one hundred and eighty-nine pounds in their six feet frame laboured up behind him, not for the first time I smiled, remembering the advice of the *South American Handbook* to 'try and look as little like a tourist as possible'.

Two campesinos passed, a pickaxe sticking out of one of their bundles. We wished each other good-day. They smiled as I hammed up my exhaustion, then carried on effortlessly climbing.

'And then you work?' I shouted after them in hoarse astonishment.

'Cada dia. Each day.'

A middle-aged woman passed me, laden. I watched her knotted calves rise and fall below her heavy, woollen dress. One bend further on she stopped, plucked a plant and signalled that I should breathe it. It was for '¡El corazon!' and she thumped her heart.

When I reached the spot, I breathed in the herb's mint/ammonia vapours and stared over the landscape. It took a couple of minutes for my breathing to steady. I would have been useless in the Inca army, covering their network of roads up and down the Andes from Ecuador to Chile. There was always a war on somewhere in Inca Peru and all young men had to serve their time.

A huge, broad-winged, red-backed hawk, mouse in beak, soared into view. I watched it rise on the air currents, becoming a marker for the height I was at; the space I looked across. In other civilisations such space was left for hawks alone. Not in the Andes.

Carl Sandburg wrote, in a poem called 'At the Gates of Tombs':

> If any fool, babbler, gabby mouth, stand up and say
> Let us make a civilisation, where the sacred
> and beautiful things of toil and genius shall last –
> slew him in as a lifer at San Quentin.

But it was not so easy to be dismissive of the Incas. Throughout the Andes their toil and genius had been cut into the land itself. Here as in the Colca I looked over a valley where utility and design had given the landscape rhythm – row upon row of perfect terraces, smoothed and buttressed, rising to the highest, green handkerchief.

When finally I made the summit, my throat parched, my thigh muscles trembling, the herb woman was waiting. She held out a Coca-Cola to me.

'¿Gaseosa?' By her side, a pile of bottles of Coca-Cola and Inca-Kola lay on a blanket. I paid and gulped.

'¿Cada dia?' I asked her too.

'Si, Es mi trabajo. My work.'

Two small girls with almond-shaped Inca eyes wanted to press another gaseosa on me. I refused but gave them a couple of biscuits and to their delight took their photographs. They told me they were on holiday today and shyly peeped round great blocks of stone as I climbed on to the hitching post of the sun, the most sacred place in the temple. The Incas believed they could harness the power of Inti, the sun, to them and each temple had its hitching post, a small column compared to the huge masonry surrounding it, but sacred.

And for that reason most were destroyed by the Spanish invaders.

To the Incas hell was a subterranean, cold place where you lived on stones: heaven was with the sun. I lay back and turned my face to it. Briefly I held its glow through half shut eyes, felt its warmth concentrate on my upturned face. (In spite of the light breeze I would pay for this indulgence. At this altitude there is no screening from the sun's rays. For weeks I would pull slivers of skin like rice-paper from the top of my head and my ears.) No wonder, I thought, children draw the sun so much bigger than we see it. Is it not unlikely, incredible, that this gold coin, dwarfed by the space that surrounds it, can be the power-house for all life? Is it not indeed a cause for constant wonder and worship?

> My sun, the golden garden of your hair
> Has begun to flame
> And the fire has spread over our corn-fields.
>
> Already the green ears are parched
> Passed by the presence of your breath
> And the last drop of their sweat is wrung from them.
>
> Strike us with the rain of your arrows.
> Open to us the door of your eyes.
> Oh sun, source of beneficent light.
> *Quechua.*

The path to the next set of ruins was steeper and less travelled than the previous one. It turned sharply, giving panoramic views over the valley, but fell away beyond the wildflowers into nothingness. I edged my way along clutching the banking, till a young man in a bright red T-shirt and a small boy with a grey sack, who I had seen skipping up the path earlier, forced me to adopt a more dignified, upright position.

'Peligroso, eh?' I ventured.

'Oh, it gets more so,' the man advised. I noticed he was carrying something wrapped in a cloth and could only have used one hand for balance. I raised my eyes heavenwards.

'There's a tunnel up ahead but you must skirt round it. It's not too bad.' And they were off again.

I had reached optimum trust in my balance and my feet. *Know thyself*. I saw a broken ribbon of rock across empty space. No thanks.

I returned to my base temple, bought a Coke from one of the girls whose face lit up at another biscuit; and chatted with the fleet-of-foot, richly named Flavio Chuquiwillca Huallpa and his boy companion. It was difficult to breathe up there but, far from the tourist pressures of Cuzco, it was easy to talk – any silence was filled with looking.

'Wonderful view.'

'Yes, I'm Peruvian and this is my first time. The air – puro, puro.' He tensed his chest demonstratively. 'People here live long, ninety to a hundred years. They have their health because the air is so pure.

'Me? I'm Quechua, but I don't want to work as hard as they must do. The campesinos are exploited. Everything they grow they must take to the market to survive, but everything is expensive for them and so they have nothing. I think if we went back to the Inca ways, things would get better. We could be like the Japanese without the technology. Seriously. You see how well things grow up here; you see the size of the corn. Well, we could grow fruit trees; fruits that people would pay a lot for, not just maize and potatoes.'

Were there mountains like these in Scotland? What about Scottish agriculture? I translated as well as I could a Scottish strath with its green basin, and the heather slopes rising from it lost to rabbits and sheep and rock. I told him about subsidies and the situation of the crofters. He nodded understanding. A thick mop of black hair over a man-boy's smooth olive complexion. What did he do now?

'Me? I went to university for five years' study. After, everyone went into a profession. Not me. I don't want to be a robot, to live in a city. I came back here to learn music. I play in a group called Inkariy, the charango.' And he unwrapped this small, hunchbacked instrument from its covering shawl. Its polished frets shone in the sun.

He had played in Spain but after a car accident had come back here to recuperate. Yet it was hard to make a good living here as the Peruvians did not seem to like their own music. 'They prefer rock and roll. In Bolivia,' he assured me, 'it's different. People take their music seriously there.' Still, it was good to be back. Was he not Quechua with an Inca name which meant lanza sagrada, sacred lance? And the air: 'puro! puro! puro!' He always felt good here. Everywhere he went running, running, running; and on the spot he mimed it. He had brought his charango just in case of inspiration. Would he play for me?

He bent over the small instrument. Despite its size his playing was intensely physical, his involvement total. The notes hovered in the still air as he played a lament then errupted into a dance rhythm. It was a serendipitous moment of real privilege. The young boy, also a gaseosa seller, smiled with me.

'Shall we go down together?' Flavio invited.

'Oh, no. Thank you. I'd either hold you up – or die!' He laughed, tucked the charango under his arm and ran off down the track.

I shouted goodbye and soon followed at my own pace, leaving the sacred hitching post of the sun in the custody of two girls, a man lying on his back in the grass, the gaseosa-selling woman and a tethered goat.

From the small town of Urubamba the fifty kilometres' journey from Pisac to Ollantaytambo was in a colectivo so packed it was difficult to see anything. With one foot on the platform and the other hovering over the stairwell, I had to draw myself in with real concentration at every stop when the driver came round to unjam the 'automatic' door. Yet typically it was a journey not of niggle and frustration but full of accommodation, friendliness and amusement: a kind of 'in and out the dusty bluebells' played with bulging sacks.

Stooping, what I saw of the valley were glimpses of a richly farmed landscape and a dark brown river, all imbued with a hazy crepuscular Tuscan light. Ahead children lay like bundles of clothing on the edge of the road, only rolling away at the last hoot.

In the early morning, from the height of the fortress of Ollantaytambo, such a gentle Mediterranean idyll was mocked. The fortress commanded a view up the narrow valley of the Yucay River, as it wound past the ancient Inca town tucked in the crux of the mountains, before it became the turbulent Urubamba.

The night before in the main plaza I had loitered beneath a canopy which had held table football and prize shooting to the pound of rock music. Clutches of spirited teenagers had ignored me. It could have been almost anywhere; though the narrow, cold-shouldering streets, whose blank walled houses were built on Inca foundations to make corral enclosures, had felt proprietorial, eerily watchful in the darkness.

Daylight brought the darker, more powerful gods out of hiding.

As I clambered up the ranks of steep terraces, keeping an eye on my train time, early mist still clung to the bare mountainous knives of rock, and the mountain that the fortress itself stood on was festooned with dark trailing grasses like seaweed, adding to its otherworldliness. It was here that the Incas, under Manco Capac, staged their most successful defiance of the Spaniards in 1536, flooding the plain below to hamper Hernando Pizarro's horsemen.

At its top stood the unfinished Temple of the Moon: including six reddish monoliths the size of upended trucks knit by narrow columns of stone. The effort involved in any age would be awesome; it was even more so when you considered the Incas had never invented even the simplest machine for cutting stone or lifting blocks from one place to another. Instead they relied on forcing dry wedges of wood into existing cracks in the stone and pouring water on the wood to make it swell and eventually crack the stone. Cutting stone was done with a rope dipped in wet sand and used like a saw.

Other lesser giant stones still lay, waiting. In the most impressive Inca ruins I had seen, the stones did not seem toppled; the remains had too much dignity for that. No irony of Ozymandias here. Rather they appeared to be just incomplete or abandoned. True in this case! The Colla Indians from Lake Titicaca deserted the job halfway through.

They had left it for me to finish alone on a chill blue, lonely morning five centuries later. But first, watching my time, I must run my hands over the edges of the blocks, must do a sun dance on top of one, pee from another, photograph the rest, and send thrilled gibberish to the lookout posts somehow built on to the sheer rock face across the valley.

*

In my mind I am climbing higher into the past, climbing higher towards Machu Picchu. In fact Cuzco is several hundred metres higher than it. And when I bribe a willing campesina to buy a train ticket for me – gringo tourists are not supposed to use cheap local transport but to stick together on the ninety dollar tourist train – I shall be continuing a gentle descent into the lushly green Urubamba valley that, eighty kilometres beyond the small town of Aguas Calientes, becomes thick, matted jungle; becomes a hideout for Sendero.

Machu Picchu

There were five in our party for the heights of Machu Picchu – two Australians, a French couple and myself. In drizzling darkness we walked along the railway line which split the small claustrophobic town of Aguas Calientes and, a stumbling three-quarters of an hour later, began to climb the earth path from the station of Puente Ruinas. For the two steep kilometres up the muddy mountain path the rain was relentlessly Scottish. Every hundred metres or so when we met the road zigzagging its six kilometres to the top we turned to the landscape: huge conical mountains with valleys that knit together as neatly as in a child's drawing. All were matted with puffs of trees; the bright thread of a waterfall was laid over one, a snail's silver trail; and one was crossed by a great rift that made it appear a giant's helter-skelter. They changed by the minute as the clouds crossed them; the clouds themselves, impenetrable mass or the wispiest of vapours. And then, quite suddenly free from all the thick, dark vegetation which had once reclaimed the mountain-top, the first buildings were there.

In small measure each visitor must feel some of the excitement of Hiram Bingham, the North American who 'discovered' Machu Picchu on 24 July 1911. Bingham thought he had discovered Vilcabamba, the last refuge of the Incas, thus giving a romantic conclusion to his archaeological studies of the Inca civilisation. However, subsequent archaeologists proved him mistaken, seeing in Machu Picchu an important agricultural centre serving Cuzco; others speculated that it may have been a religious centre, where handmaidens for the sun god lived. Whatever its original purpose may have been, as with any ruin, we must hack from it the thick vegetation which threatens to cut it off from us: to find in it something of significance for ourselves.

We dried off as best we could at the expensive on-site tourist hotel and, as the mist rose and a pale sun came out, paid our money and entered the site itself.

My first response was an involuntary whoop of delight – 'Ayee, ayee, ayee! Mach-u Picch-u!' – which scattered my companions. We all made our own way up the stone steps to the guardian's hut, a recommended viewing point for the classic view over Machu Picchu's maze of empty plazas, chambers, alleyways, and staircases carved out of solid rock.

It was still early; the tourist train from Cuzco would not be arriving for another two hours. There was only a handful of tourists and a few gardeners in orange overalls and hard yellow hats batting the undergrowth down and checking the stonework. Soon I was alone, sitting overlooking the site, the sun warm on my back at last. My initial, extravagant cry had soon passed. I felt now a tightness in my chest instead; the old displaced feelings of worship that come when words fall before wonder.

The ancient city was compact as a walnut, or a ship pitched like an ark on the saddle of the mountain-top. A white fist of cloud enclosed and released the huge slab of Huayna Picchu which rose up behind it. Around it the dipping sea of vegetation changed to a different hue of green as the light changed: rogue rainbows bridged chasms then dissolved in the warming air.

As I turned I saw no mark that the Incas had left on this landscape, beyond the forty-five terraces leading up to the thatched hut that I counted before they all became a blur. Nor in its construction was it oppressive like Sacsayhuaman. Though there were huge stones involved, they knitted into a whole which spoke of the possibility of life; intimate, ordinary life. When I climbed down, unhurriedly making for the Temple and the Sacred Hitching Post of the Sun, I was amongst houses with gable ends, in narrow streets and lanes; in a place that had a human dimension.

I entered one of the roofless, small dwellings. The thick stone walls were not awesomely perfect here, but a combination of the found and the finished that any dyker would appreciate. There was a stout lintel over the small trapezoidal windows and door; a thoroughly familiar smell of damp moss and fern. On a hundred occasions I have idled similarly in a deserted croft in the Highlands of Scotland and wondered about the lives that had been lived in it.

In the Sacred Plaza also the ghosts were accommodating. Alpaca, with their short necks the most sheepish of llamas, kept the grass down, picking next to the grey, mossed stone. In the stillness there was the buzz of bees, bird sound – royal bluebirds darted all around the mountain – the hum of the Urubamba twisting far below. The Incas never invented the wheel so the lived-in city must have known similar muffled sounds: soft, trotting llamas and the chatter of people in the streets. The tourists crossing the grassy space now were respectfully quiet, smiling, as if walking down the nave of a vast cathedral. I wondered what it must be like to work in such an atmosphere.

A stocky man, dressed in rough denim with a whistle round his neck to warn off the unthinking, stood just beyond the ruined walls of the Temple of the Sun; on the periphery of everyone's intense looking. His closed fist shot to his mouth from time to time, followed by a few slow chews.

'You work here?'

'Sí.'

'¿Cada dia? It must be good for the soul.'

He nodded but seemed reluctant to expand; his face expressionless.

I smiled self-consciously and turned away. Then he was behind me, showing me a good place to take a photograph, using his whistle as the camera. We climbed up the steps to intihuatana, the hitching post of the sun. More camera tips, but I had run out of film and mimed to avoid denting his enthusiasm.

'You have a map?' he asked. I showed him the relevant page of my guide-book. He grunted dismissively. 'Mapa Español. No. Mapa Inca. Inca.'

He led me to a large, upright scallop of rock. He pointed to Huayna Picchu; he pointed to a chisel of rock. He pointed across at Cerro Machu Picchu; he pointed to a curving breast. *There* was the road to Cuzco. *There* was the Vilcanota (the Quechua name for the Urubamba). The sun came this way – through the Gates of the Sun, crossing the temple, to intihuatana – here.

'Ah, yes,' I said. 'Yes, I see . . . You are a bit Inca, yes?'

'Sí.' Strong and deep.

'You believe in the sun?'

'Sí. El papa – el sol.'

'And the earth?'

'La tierra – mi madre. Mama tierra. El agua – mi madre. La luna – mi madre.'

'And the stars?'

'Eyes. Have you not seen young girls with eyes like stars?'

'But only the sun is papa?'

'Sí. Solamente el sol es mi padre.'

He spoke slowly, deliberately, first in the music of Quechua then in Spanish, or Castellano as he called it, stopping to emphasise his points with a jabbing, rhetorical 'eh-eh?' The lines on his forehead and round the top of his nose looked chiselled in mahogany, as if his face had not been aged but tempered through the centuries. His round, brown eyes regarded me obliquely, a little suspiciously above the high cheekbones. But the winking smile we had shared over 'las chicas con ojos como estrellas' had loosened him up.

'Do you think life here was hard for the Incas?'

'No. For the Incas, easy. Many paths; they run everywhere, chewing coca.' And he danced a run: 'Corriendo, corriendo, poo-poo-poo.'[1]

'Would you have liked to live in Inca times?'

'Sí. Incas work hard, but they eat well. Papas, maize, alpaca, puma, condors. Life for the Incas was good.' He whistled now and tinkled an imaginary drum, before offering me three teeth of golden maize.

Standing with him, chewing the chalky corn, it was not difficult to enter his vision of the only past to which he could comfortably look; a spiritual homeland to which he could never return. When they planted the fields back then, one field was for Inti, the sun god, one for the Inca and the third for the *ayllu* (a clan forming part of the community; normally there were four *ayllus* in a village). In an empire where no one was his own master except the Inca, was it socialism or a dictatorship which prevailed? Whatever, my guide saw dignity and a full stomach.

The spirit of brotherhood travels not only from country to country but also from time to time. In Machu Picchu, the most stunning, the most friendly ruin, where all elements of Inca society – the powerful, the religious, the military, the workforce – shared the same mountain-top, one hoped in harmony, I could imagine a niche for my Inca guide – and, almost, for myself.

---

[1] with feet of thunder they trod the thinning mists
    and touched the earth and the stones
    until they could recognise them in the night or in death.
                    The Heights of Machu Picchu: Pablo Neruda.

When I come to visit you
Do not fling me from your house
In my misery.

Sun, my father, moon, my mother,
You might look at my face
Where the tears of blood run down.

Quechua.

We each make our own Inca trails, whether it be the walking route of
that name which brings you to Machu Picchu spectacularly through
the Gates of the Sun; the halting journey I made by bus, colectivo
and train; or the tourists' ninety dollar day trip on a special train.
The experience as far as I could gather never disappoints: because
of its own unique qualities, but also because of the attention we all
pay it. For Machu Picchu is the closest I have come to a Mecca, a
once-in-my-lifetime destination and, like the route to Mecca, each
Inca trail has deep and hidden roots in a life long before one pins
Cuzco on the map.

Before I left the fortress, in the late afternoon I climbed once more
up to the guardian's hut to say goodbye. I had achieved what I came
to Peru to do and, more than I could realise, this was to be the end
of something. I had wanted to hold its stillness, its mystery to me.
I had never asked my guide but if I had I am sure he would have
answered, 'Machu Picchu – mi madre.'

That the experience was an intense one for all was obvious from
the babel of voices on the road down. When you have shared
something like that, you want to find out a little more about those
who have shared it with you. And now our small party showed
the same intimacy I had witnessed in all the random groupings I
had seen with a recent experience of Machu Picchu behind them.
Enough of the heights! Let the road run beneath us for a while.
Where do you live? Is it a good place to live? And your job? Your
girlfriend? Do you think you'll ever get married?

The French guy worked as a chauffeur in Paris and his girlfriend
did anything while they saved to travel – America, Africa and now
here. At Puente Ruinas she lost her glasses and we all searched for
them as if she had been our lifelong friend. One of the Australians
worked in real estate in Hong Kong: 'The toughest place to deal
in the whole world.' He was in Peru for a fortnight with his tall,
red-cheeked friend, a.k.a. The Checked Sports Jacket. Later in a

restaurant in Cuzco, the estate agent, leaning into him, began to count: 'Miriam, now she was twenty-four, Dolores twenty-five; which makes Freda number twenty-six . . .'

But on the packed train back to Cuzco we were all still soul-mates. A family who lived there befriended us, looked after our bags and, solicitous of each other, we took turns on the one spare seat from which they had moved a child. As we descended through the darkness into Cuzco on an endless series of switchbacks, their daughter asked each of us to sing a song for her from our own countries. My mouth still slightly bitter from chewing a coca leaf a campesino had thrust on me, I sang the 'Skye Boat Song' softly to her smile and she sang a love song about a bird. Shakily, she printed in my notebook, 'CON CARIÑO DE KUKULI' (with love from Kukuli). Kukuli was Quechua for 'beautiful bird' and even in the dim light of the carriage I could see she had eyes like stars.

The Sting
CUZCO AIRPORT

In Cuzco International Airport, the 'queue' for the flight to Puerto Maldonaldo, gateway to the jungle, swelled before me: a snake that had gorged itself over and over. Whole families sat on bundles and sacks as if camped out or ready for evacuation. In Peru distances are so vast and the terrain can be so formidable that aeroplanes are not a luxury, but often the only shakily effective means of passing between desert, mountain and jungle.

I put my bags between my feet to feel them with my legs, and took out my flight ticket. It was still early morning and, having been unable to confirm my flight by phone (surprise, surprise), I was relieved to be here in good time. Rattling to the airport in a taxi after despairing of the scheduled bus, I had felt a free-floating grumpiness, a symptom of the thin layers of anxiety which I had found coat the start of any journey in Latin America. But, I told myself, by the time you are standing at the airport terminal (not the train or the bus station), you have burned off the top ones and, come on, lad, you can afford to relax a little.

And I did not want to rush this hour, not with Machu Picchu behind me; the rainforest ahead: two great wings that would beat in my memory. I held my ticket tightly to me and smiled at the thought. Yet in a country where the pull of the past is so strong and the future so tantalising, it is best when you are travelling to live exclusively in the present.

There is a tap on my shoulder and some mumbled words. I do not catch the sense at first. Then: 'Your back – sucio – dirty.' I turn round to see a trail of spit running down the length of my left shoulder-blade. It must have happened around the glass doors on the way in. Some poor gringo-hater. I thank the man, a campesino, and pull off my top to wipe away the gob with toilet roll. How far

59

does the man help me? I cannot remember but I do recall thinking he must be sharing my feelings of pity and anger at whoever felt a need to make their mark in such a way.

I get the worst off; the light, silvery smears will have to be scrubbed off later. I feel my face is still pinched with disgust when I look at my feet. My shoulder-bag is gone!

A scream begins deep inside me, a scream coming through a big, empty place, deep as the Colca Canyon, arid as the Nazca Desert, where nothing can give it comfort. And as it grows inside me so it gathers to itself all the reasons why such a bitter thing should not, cannot be. Thousands upon thousands of words; image upon image upon image. Time buckles and I am skewered to this one moment. But the scream only comes in a series of small, desperate gasps: 'Oh God, no no no. Please, Jesus, Jesus, no.'

I look frantically from dark-skinned, blank face to blank face – a stranger in a strange, impassive land. '¡Mi bolso! ¡Mi bolso!' One woman waves her hand that-a-way. I take a few steps then, remembering my hold-all, push my way back to it like a drowning man. I swing it over my shoulder and run aimlessly, blindly round the airport floor. Now it is busier and difficult to tell where one queue ends, another begins. But there are the two German girls, Ulriche and Betti, waiting for a flight to Lima. 'I've just been robbed! My bag, my writing, my camera, films – they got it all!' Lord, don't let it be me speaking. What do they reply? We hug and I rush off. Other gringos stand over their rucksacks: it's like watching a road accident. Relief. But suddenly a squat campesina is waving me to follow her. 'Oh God, please. Please.' She scuttles towards the door with me at her shoulder. We are running down the side of the building now towards a stack of fat sacks, the perfect place to dispose of what the thieves don't want. 'Jesus, please, if not the camera, the films, please the notebooks. The notebooks . . .'

I picture the few campesinos who guard the sacks moving away as we approach. I can see the black-backed notebooks, stuffed down between the sacks like something lost in a hayloft. She will not understand my joy when I hug her; when I dance and crush their hands with gratitude.

'Please – the notebooks.'

Suddenly she stops and turns, calling to someone behind me. 'You mean, it's not me you want?' She laughs like a horse. Too cruel. And I am much too disappointed to curse her, to realise that she is probably in for a cut herself.

There were no policemen on the floor of the airport. Rumour, the Reuters of Peru, had it that they were all fighting terrorists. But on the second landing I found small groups of them with machine-guns lazily overlooking the booking hall.

I was shown into a bare room where paper spilled from the desks then taken back round the main hall. But I could tell no more than I have written here and I think they all knew from the start it was hopeless. A policeman asked a few people in the queue questions which they answered desultorily. Later a hastily assembled identification parade of three sat before me. Poor sullen-faced campesinos shifting uneasily on their seats. I could not tell if any of them had been involved but pleaded with them: 'If you know anything, please tell. It's the notebooks I want back. For the rest I don't care.' They were so removed from guilt or caring their denials were the merest bemused shrug.

A young policeman in a leather jacket painfully, letter by letter, typed my losses on an ancient machine.

Notebook. Black. 300 pages. Full.

Notebooks. Red covers. Poems.

Notebook. Machu Picchu on the cover. A play.

'And what else?' he asked excitedly, as if I was short-changing him. 'What else?' I listed all the things I could remember: camera, five films, pens, pencils, compass, maps, books, address book etc. 'But it's the notebooks that are important. Soy un escritor.'

Other policemen drifted in. 'El es escritor.' Their hands said it all: sympathy, hopelessness. Mala suerte. Bad luck.

'But do you think there's a chance? Do you?' I was running beside the young detective who carried my bag on his shoulder towards the waiting and very late plane.

'Yes, surely there's a chance. Seguro.' I held his arm tightly as we ran. He was hope and I needed his touch.

On the steps up to the plane a group of irate Peruvians waved tickets as the embattled stewardess tried to explain that there were no seats. I pushed past – calamity kills scruple – and explained that I was late because I had been robbed. A steward with grey hair and neat moustache waved me rather wearily into the cockpit where the pilot and co-pilot were carrying on a violently gestured argument which was to last all the way to Puerto Maldonaldo.

After take-off, a miracle I might have thought in other circumstances, the stewardess handed me a sickly sweet fruit drink and I tried to peer through the tight lattice of scratch marks on the window at the Andes, at the snow, at the jungle. But all I saw was what I had lost. Wide-eyed as any of the cockpit's meaningless dials, I flew over the most spectacular scenery, feeling nothing more than the pain from my broken wings.

PART TWO

Travels with my angst.

Lost in the Rainforest
TAMBOPATA

The forest was cool where we walked a hundred feet below the canopy. Here only five per cent of the light filters through. For that reason the leaves are large but tapered, so the frequent rain falls from them and does not engender fungal growths. In a few days' time the President of the Society for the Protection of the Selva Sur, David Ricalde, would tell me, 'Some of these naturalists, it's not their fault but they don't know their stuff. I mean, I think if someone is showing you the rainforest and he doesn't stop every ten yards to show you something, then that's not a good guide. If he doesn't stop every fifty yards, well, I don't know but there's something very wrong.'

Chris Sharpe, a smiling, sensitive biologist from Leeds, here for as long as he could stay to study primates, passed the test easily. Desperately I tried to hold down the rising sickness I felt about the theft of my writing to listen to all he was telling. The other two in the party were an Australian and an Englishman, both in their mid-twenties and both stiffly uncommunicative. We had sailed up the brown Tambopata forty kilometres south from Puerto Maldonaldo in a skiff that barely cleared the water. I had asked the Englishman, who was tilting his clean-cut face to the sun, if I could use some of his sun cream, seizing the opportunity to talk about my robbery. There were disgusted nods, but little sense of sympathy from either. It turned out the Australian's baggage with much expensive equipment had never arrived in Quito, not even made it to the continent (or so he'd been told), and I sensed he had no sympathy left for any other's misfortune. When I asked him about the Galapagos T-shirt he was wearing, he merely snapped, 'No, I haven't been. The T-shirt was cheap.' His gingerish stubble I imagined was not a natural growth but a product of choleric distemper.

They had met each other on some trip early on their travels and been together ever since: two people cutting their own swathe through the continent. They were here 'for the nature' – everything else was just blameful hassle. Particularly the people. The English-man told me that if someone came up to him in a queue he would punch him in the face. It was the most feeling I saw in him, apart from when describing some bitter wrangle in the London ad agency which had caused his walk-out and propelled him here.

Decomposition in the rainforest is quick. You can put your finger through the bark and into the flesh of a huge fallen tree after four months. In Britain an oak would take twenty years to reach such a state. (Repeat: 'Decomposition in the rainforest is quick. You can put your finger through the bark and into the flesh of a huge fallen tree after four months. In Britain an oak would take twenty years . . .' Hang on in there, boy!) Here, ants and fungi race to make the most of good, organic matter and the rotting trunks themselves play host to an assortment of bright green epiphytes. In no time at each treefall saplings and ferns sprout in the shallow crater left by the spread of the roots. A line from a Bob Dylan song came to mind: 'Those not busy bein' born are busy dyin'.'

Chris pointed out the strange-looking stilt palm, its dangerously spiked stilts 'walking' the tree towards sunlight. He told us the story of the lapuna tree, the mother of the forest. When it was chopped down it became the Amazon, its branches the many tributaries. He showed us the shewanakoo, a teaching tree for shamans that menstruating women must not pass.

The rainforest is a tightly knit ecosystem but one that is only vaguely understood; which is why damage to any part of it can never be exactly limited. As an example of symbiosis Chris showed us a tangarana tree which has an accommodation with ants. The tree houses them and they in return protect it from creepers and other crawlers. Tap its bark and out they come. It is a test of a young shaman to be strapped to this tree.

> O strap me to a Tangarana tree,
> a Tangarana tree, a Tangarana tree,
> O strap me to a Tangarana tree,
> but give me back . . .

The forest opened at Laguna Chica, a perfect oxbow lake. The first creature we had seen, a small turtle, was sunning itself on a rock as we climbed into a canoe and paddled and drifted round the green-speared edge of the lake. In the perfect silence we heard a toucan's grating call. Hoatzin, primitive-looking birds once thought to be related to archaeopterix, flopped between branches, their ochre crests like Mohican head-dresses. Red-capped cardinals flitted from branch to light branch.

The richness of wildlife here, as Barry had told me, is legion. As a leaflet of the Tambopata Reserve Society (TReeS), founded in 1986, informs: 'In terms of biological diversity, the forests of Madre de Dios are the richest in the world. Research at Tambopata over the last ten years has shown that the Reserve has more species of birds (over 570), butterflies (1,200) and many other animal groups than any other location of its size on earth.' But such facts are both exciting and misleading. For one thing, at twenty square miles Tambopata provides only half the territory required by an adult jaguar; for another, wildlife is wisely shy. One listens for and looks for the signs of a presence – a call, a disorder in the green face of the forest signalling a monkey's passage – and most times one must be satisfied with that. To believe the brochures, or for that matter the cover of the *South American Handbook* with its exotic bright orange cock of the rock (Rupicola rupicola), is to be disappointed.

Still, Laguna Chica itself was so beautiful in its tranquillity that my heart could not help but lift. Then, just as we were tying up the canoe, came the first heavy spats of rain on the leaves and with a roll of thunder the heavens opened. We all tipped our paper valuables into Chris's waterproof bag and tramped in mud back to base. The driving force of the rain precluded conversation, sealed each of us in with his own thoughts. Mine were of that last tropical downpour in Samaná when the potential violence had seemed so distant to me. I felt far more threatened now.

My only pen had stopped working at the start of the walk; in the rain my watch face went blank. 'I'm getting a bit *pissed off* with this!' I shouted against the wall of white noise to three deaf backs. The date was April the first and it didn't end a minute too soon.

I do not sleep though. At dinner the two cholerics carried on a huddled conversation while I sat at the end of the row feeling the cutlery might melt in my hands. Now I cannot bear the darkness and have to keep on relighting the candle, fumbling for the matches in the total darkness. I feel I have nothing: no one to talk to, nothing personal to act as a comforter – not a photograph, not a letter: *nada*. I remember again sitting in the airline office in Lima, chanting to myself the lines of Elizabeth Bishop, 'The art of losing isn't hard to master', and tapping my shoulder-bag, thinking, this is the important one. Already I had had presentiments of the satisfaction I would feel when I eventually got the bag home – the huge relief as I unpacked my treasures. Now in the night its contents come back to me randomly, though it will be some weeks before, as a way of exorcism, I can make

A KIND OF INVENTORY

of the bag itself   an expensive beautiful heavy canvas camera bag with leather trimmings   a thick canvas strap with a suede lining   a Christmas present from my sister and brother-in-law especially for my trip   at first I was concerned, mmm, I thought, a camera bag   looks rather too expensive but it was so practical and I could organise my material so effectively in it   this is how I did it

main compartment   poetry notebook   play notebook camera sunglasses *South American Handbook*, later withdrawn under pressure from notebooks   pewter flask   a gift from my friend Jack with Edinburgh Castle on one side and the Scott Monument on the other   it was sleeved in the pink silk pouch Julie had made for me and embroidered LIVE IT LOVE IT WRITE IT   a large shiny brown seed from Samaná

in the small side compartments   malaria pills five films, three rolls of 36 exposed   a small black travel alarm bought for a trip to the USSR   a collection of poetry I was translating signed by Washington Delgado   photocopies of all important documents

in the zipped front compartments   my black-covered journal when it was full 300 pages I moved it to the inside replacing the *South American Handbook* to my luggage and inserted a fresh one   material for correspondence postcards of Dumfries and Galloway a booklet with addresses of British Council offices

my pencil case   black heavy plastic it poppered shut and when open had spaces for pens like medical instruments   a pentel pencil my nephew Michael had given me two Christmases

ago   a clicker pencil Alastair Reid had given me in Samaná
a clicka pencil I had bought myself four ball points   inside the
zipped part of this case a small St Christopher a small boy had
given my mother many years before   turquoise blue, still in
its original cellophane wrapper   a lucky horseshoe from my
mother   a lucky plastic bull from my father who suddenly
felt he should give me something lucky too a piece of lucky
heather from my English department colleagues an antique brass
compass from my uncle

in two small front pockets   my black address book   a red
and green notebook with contact addresses in Lima, La Paz, San
Paolo, Porto Allegre and various notes   a small calendar with
pictures of Scottish landscapes   a lollipop a Paddington Bear
puzzle   these last were items forming part of a South American
Survival Kit from my English department   a small fruit knife
with a pearl handle still in its Jenners cardboard box which my
father had dug out of his drawer for me   a small pocket book I
had filled with addresses and notes

in the zipper compartment on the cover   maps of South
America Hispaniola   street maps of New York and Lima; letters
of introduction from Canongate the Scottish Arts Council the British
Council   good-luck cards, letters, photographs.

The art of losing's not too hard to master
though it may look like (Write it!) like disaster.

The next morning, unslept, I was up at five, but because of rain it
was much later when we started the six kilometres' trail to the larger
lake on the reserve.

I had nothing to do but paddle, and my fingers blistered as we
canoed around Laguna Grande while the Australian, crouched in
the bow with his bazooka lens, shook his head and tutted at
each audible paddle stroke. Both he and the Englishman were
collecting 'worth-it' shots.

'Take your own pace back to the lodge,' Chris said and marched
off, a slight figure in butchered jeans and a torn striped shirt
like a huge smock; a long feather of hair down his neck. But I
felt I could not lose him and hung on the hour-and-a-half walk
firing the occasional question like a lifeline, till he succumbed to
a conversation about the war poets: 'like old beggars under sacks
. . . we cursed through sludge . . .'

'You're still there, aren't you?' Chris asked at lunch. I nodded mutely. 'You must forget it. Or else you're going to lose this too . . .' But afterwards, I found myself in the dim bathroom of my hut staring at a haunted face. Over and over again I thought of the robbery. Brick by brick my despair built.

'La cabeza debe regir a la corazon. The head must rule the heart,' Mario Ortiz, who was passing through Tambopata, had pronounced, eying me gravely but sympathetically and tapping his head and heart in turn. Oh please, not Hemingway's 'grace under pressure', I thought, I'm crap at all that; and now circumstances have found me out far more comprehensively than Petra's eagle stare ever could. I too am a lost, insecure Colin, my feelings of togetherness an illusion. Bugger 'writing in interesting places'. I want my desk!

Marcia had lived in the jungle for nine years. A native of Los Angeles, she had been an exporter of craft goods from Lima when, on a short trip to the jungle, her plane was grounded at Puerto Maldonaldo for two weeks. 'It was the rainy season and the runway hadn't been concreted at that time,' she explained. While waiting for a flight she was asked to do some translating at one of the jungle lodges. At the end of two weeks she was hooked. She flew back to Lima and wrote to all her clients telling them not to expect any more craft goods: she was quitting and going to work in the jungle. She was now manager of Explorers Inn and gave all the new arrivals the same breezy, Californian smile of welcome.

'I rarely leave the jungle now; certainly not with pleasure. It's so interesting, so-o-o mysterious, you're always learning something.' But she gave no impression of being a recluse. There was a story that she had once been married to a hollow cheeked Indian tour guide called Willy Wither who had taken us up the river and touchingly offered me the use of his very expensive camera ('A holiday without a camera is a terrible thing.'), but I could see no special contact between them. Slim in her dungarees, with her long, curly, chestnut hair and wide-eyed enthusiasm, some would tell you Marcia was 'a little cookie', but I saw someone who had the wisdom to recognise where she was happy and the courage to act on it. Her contentment had nurtured a generous soul.

It was generosity and wisdom I was after when I climbed up the steps to her small office which was set apart from the larger huts in the forest clearing. I climbed hesitantly, feeling clumsy as the tame macaw which that morning had taken my fingernails for a bunch of nuts.

'I'm afraid,' I told her, 'I'm going to crack up. I feel I've lost everything; that I may just as well go home.'

'Oh, don't despair yet. There's still a chance of the stuff turning up; not the camera, but the notebooks, yes.'

'You really think so?' Impossible straws. Better to accept it's all gone. Gone.

'Yeah, and besides, there's a lot more of South America to see and a lot of work you can still do in two months.' She seemed to light up at the idea.

'Yes, well. Perhaps I'll go for a walk in the forest and see if I can sort something out.'

'Do that. It would be terrible if you lost this opportunity. And you know,' she added, 'the forest soothes.'

The forest soothes.

There was a tree in it whose story I did not tire of hearing. One afternoon in the main lodge, surrounded by displays about rainforest life and conservation, I talked to Richard, a rangy, bespectacled botanist, studying Why Trees Fall.

TOM: You know what's amazed me most of all that I've seen is Big Tree.

RICHARD: Ah, yes.

TOM: Tell me the story again.

RICHARD: Well, it's a seed from the fig family, a strangler fig, and it attaches itself . . .

TOM: How big's the seed?

RICHARD: Oh, say three-quarters of an inch – a thumbnail. Anyway, as I was saying, it attaches itself to a tree.

TOM: Any tree? Which tree?

RICHARD: Well, a lapuna if you like.

TOM: The mother of the forest?

RICHARD: The mother of the forest.

TOM: Yes. Chris told us the story of how the man and the woman fed from this tree and, when they were away, to get at the food others chopped it down and the trunk became the Amazon, the branches its tributaries.

RICHARD: That's the story.

TOM: Back to Big Tree.

RICHARD (No trace of a sigh): The seed germinates and sends roots down to the earth for nutrients. The roots grow huge, sculptural wings to buttress the tree and the climber wraps itself around the lapuna, which slowly decays inside it.

TOM: How long does this take?

RICHARD: No one knows.

TOM: No one! There is no way to tell how old the tree is?

RICHARD: No. Because there are no definite growing seasons in the tropics, trees don't have rings; so without actually watching them and measuring them grow, it's impossible to date them. In fact there are only about three species of tree in the rainforest that have been definitely aged, in terms of their lifespan.

TOM: Well, is there a time when Big Tree stops being a plant and starts being a tree?

RICHARD: No.

TOM: It's still a plant?

RICHARD: It's still a plant.

TOM: But isn't there some physical quality that makes a tree a tree? I don't know – woodiness?

RICHARD: Lots of shrubs have wood and they're not trees.

TOM: Ah . . . mmm . . . uh-hu . . .

RICHARD: It's too easy to get bogged down in the study of classifications. Lots of scientists do, you know. It's a problem that started with Plato and his idea of the essence of things: that there should be an *essence* of tree. But it just doesn't operate here. That's one of the reasons it's exciting for a botanist to work in the rainforest. I mean, in Britain, if I was studying the daisy family for example, there'd be the garden daisy and a few other bits and bobs, but that would be it. But if I was studying the daisy family here, I'd be looking at plants from the size of daisies as we know them, to plants the size of trees.

TOM: The size of trees!

RICHARD: Yes.

TOM: But they wouldn't be trees.

RICHARD: No. (Pause.) They'd be daisies.

Though I could see that the sun still lit the highest canopy, on the jungle floor it was already too late. I knew I was on the wrong track when the tall reeds broke to reveal the brown-bellied river. By then the map was the faintest glow in my hands, the thread of tracks unreadable. The big, light-hungry leaves were almost black now as I walked briskly back along the path searching for the track to take me back to the lodge. Presently, there was a lightening of foliage and I thought, almost disappointedly, all that panic for nothing. But the path took me back into darkness and I felt my first real twinge of panic. Stupid. Stupid. Stupid. To paddle around Laguna Chica enjoying the idle drift of time, the depth of natural silence; to go and rest my head for a last time between the fifteen-foot-high buttresses of Big Tree . . . And without a torch. What did Barry say? 'Watch for ants, falling Brazil nuts, poisonous snakes and never go anywhere after midday without a torch.' Something like that. And now here I am, stumbling as I start to jog in my heavy, muddied wellingtons along the pale grey light of a path. I call. Silence. I shout. Silence. I scream, 'Hello-o-o-o!' Silence. The foliage absorbs whatever sound I make and returns silence. As Annie Dillard tells us: this is nature's one comment. I shout and shout for all the warmth of company I'll be missing at dinner – and the sweat pours from me. Thorns snag me. A tree trunk slams into me. At last I stumble off the path into complete darkness. My feet find only forest vegetation, ground creepers. Lost. Utterly lost.

I feel around me and find a branch to sit on. I cover myself with insect repellent, have a drink of water (my two foresights). And wait.

I am strangely calm now I know my own efforts are hopeless. It is something of a relief to have let my clattering, panicking self go, to wear instead something of the forest's stillness. I am one more black silhouette in this sixty-million-year-old forest. I threaten nothing, but sit on my branch, attentive as any other creature; as slowly the forest reveals itself in the cry of a bird, the crash of a branch, the rustle of leaves as something moves through the forest litter; the incessant percussive music of insects. 'If you can,' Barry said, 'Go for a walk in the forest at night. Just find an old trunk, sit down and listen. I love it, though some people just can't handle it.' I amaze myself – I, who used to be terrified of the unlit hallway – ready to sit it out, unafraid; friends with the living darkness. But I hear a distant shout. And another. Another from a different direction. I shout back, 'Terrace Trail! Terrace Trail!' But there I was wrong.

I was found by Chris sitting not ten yards from Big Tree. No wonder I had felt so calm. Three more torchlit seekers join us. They feel like my closest friends. 'What took you so long? Lose my stuff one day, myself the next – should I be allowed out on my own?'

We are loudly human all the way back as they light up for me just how far I had strayed. When we walk out of the forest into the candlelights of the lodge, the forest moves into our spaces like the sea into scoops of sand. But, bathed in its silence, I am refreshed.

'The Richest Country in the World'
CUZCO

The green world soothed, as did the ready kindness of Chris and Marcia – the comfort of strangers. But back in Cuzco I had to fight to recall the strength I had found; force myself to remember I had been lost in a sixty-million-year-old forest but had found the still centre.

After my talk with Marcia I had tramped along the trails listening to imaginary advice from a weave of voices, the same ones I had silently and joyfully addressed at Machu Picchu. I had decided that all my stuff was irretrievably lost; that I did not want to continue my projected journey but would strike out and do something different – go to Ecuador perhaps and if possible from there into Brazil. I had felt at the instant the idea suggested itself to me the first glimmer of positive thought: suddenly I knew I was not going to sink. Thoughtlessly, grandly, I had then taken a fallen branch and lopped the top leaves off some innocent plant like a child.

I found myself hanging on to that spirit, first at the office of Policia de Investigationes del Peru (motto: 'Honor y Lealtad') where it was never the same man on my case. In fact there was not much of a feeling that anyone was on my case at all. The desks were covered with piles of paperwork, seemingly beyond classification. The fact that everything relating to my loss was scribbled in children's school jotters with cartoon covers was not exactly a boost to my confidence.

There was much coming and going and shaking of hands before a lurid calendar of a glossy, tanned blonde in a jungle setting. Immediately after my robbery I had thought all this action would be to my benefit. I remembered moving from one to the other, explaining: I am a writer; the notebooks are what is precious to me. One policeman was short and stocky, his thick, wiry hair shaped into a point at the nape of his neck. His heavy gold rings and his bomber jacket and his wide-foot stance had added up to a man of experience in my eyes. How I had welcomed his physicality, his touch: the tiniest sensation that yes, it might be all right. Today he put my loss into perspective – by ignoring me.

I waited miserably for my Certificado Numero 031, stating my losses and their circumstances, and with one last appeal – 'It's the notebooks' – vanished from their casebooks.

In New York I'd sat in the winter sun on wooden steps at South Street pier and swapped cards with an old girlfriend, now a free-lance writer. My card read "Tom Pow – teacher/writer." Somewhere I'd read that a card was an invaluable social lubricant in South America. However that may be, I was soon to discover that I was not a natural disburser of "my card", and very few people received one. I had stared over the famous landscape: the three bridges, the brownstones of Brooklyn Heights. How does one write a travel book, I'd wondered aloud, how describe the sheer physicality of life? At that moment a pigeon with a stump for one leg hirpled past. And now on the bus from the airport I could not stop noticing detail. How can I remember it all? How can I recapture the texture of my experiences? The situation was beginning to feel heavy, hopeless. I stared out of the bus window at piles of refuse on the wasteland fringes of the road. Laser eyes. Crazy.

In an attempt to counteract despondency, to reclaim the green world for itself, not solely as a balm for my despair, I arranged with Barry's help an interview with David Ricalde.

David Ricalde Rios was President of the Asociacion por la Conservacion de la Selva Sur (ACSS). The association had a tidy office in the busy Avenida del Sol. David arrived in a beige boiler-suit and trainers, fitting for his serious directness, for he was a shy man when not warmed to a subject: small-talk was not his forte. He acknowledged this when he told me in fluent English that he wanted to do a post-graduate degree in biology in the States. 'People say there are courses in the economics of wildlife management, but I think it's better to be a scientist than a talker.'

ACSS was set up by himself and interested friends five years before and he had been working on it since. (He was still classed as a volunteer, but with a wife about to give birth was rethinking his situation.) The association ran on a tight budget funded from various sources. Wildlife Conservation International had helped them make contact with interested scientists and individuals.

'We talk with thirty thousand people a year for two thousand dollars,' he said proudly, contrasting that figure with the larger, better-funded organisations.

As a trained biologist and a conservationist ('since I was nine'), it was not surprising that he was interested in the Selva Sur which boasts more plants and species than anywhere else on earth. The Tambopata Reserve, as I have said, holds world records in birds, butterflies and dragonflies. Manu National Park, which is more isolated up the Madre de Dios River, has two million insects, one thousand species of birds, fifteen thousand species of plants, two hundred species of freshwater fish, two hundred species of bats – some still unknown to science. In other words this area is the greatest celebration of nature our planet has ever known. And in the past four decades we've lost half of it. Half of it remains to be saved.

David saw ACSS as a pressure group ('Not like Greenpeace. I think it's more productive to be polite,') whose primary aim was to secure the future of the rainforest in an area stretching from the Heath Sanctuary on the Bolivian border up to and including Manu and the Tambopata Reserves: an area of one and a half million hectares, the size of Switzerland. The figure was neither excessive nor arbitrary, but the minimum size recommended to protect biological diversity. (It is worthwhile here remembering the jaguar's requirements.) Besides, Tambopata for all its world records was only protected by a resolution. Manu on the other hand was protected by a supreme decree. Both these measures were less than laws. Roads were built by law and roads 'opened up' jungles; so a constant battle of education and persuasion needed to be waged by ACSS and other pressure groups on the government.

'To me as a Peruvian,' David said, his deep, brown eyes alive with the topic, 'nationalism means Manu, means biological diversity. Nationalism is not big battles, a glorious history, but something you can feel proud of.' However, he took a broad view of the duties and responsibilities of being a scientist in Peru. 'We are realistic. We are not saying, "Oh, we must save these beautiful species!" We realise that conservation is people too. Thus a Peruvian biologist must be well trained in fieldwork, experienced in research and have an idea of priorities. In other words not see science in isolation from economics, anthropology, politics – all these disciplines should be working together.'

David's vision of turning the Tambopata Reserve Project into the most important tropical university in the world and a model of development for the protection of the rainforest in Peru, if not the world, hinged on being able to persuade government and local interests that their benefits did not lie with the destruction of the forest.

Puerto Maldonaldo, 'the biological capital of the world', was a rapidly growing town boosted by thousands of settlers from the Andes seeking fine gold dust in the rivers, to work as loggers or to become slash-and-burn farmers. Apart from the landless Andeans, the greatest damage was done by cattle ranchers whose clearance of one acre of rainforest would support 0.4 of one cow. It was a statistic such as that which proved the best weapon in ACSS's campaign. David also pointed to Explorers Inn which he claimed, on the same size of land, netted its owner a turnover of $800,000 per year: a goldmine and a transparent example of competitive land-use.

'Ecotourism,' said David, 'is a very viable alternative to rainforest destruction.[1] But the jungle lodges should do more to make contact with the local communities, to tell them what they are doing. The scientists too must be seen to be helpful. Conservation must be integrated into the local community. Instead of which too many locals see the tourists arrive in Puerto Maldonaldo and speed across it to the river without even buying a Coke. They never see the

[1] I should point out that the figures David gave me here are disputed by John Forrest of TREES who goes on to write: 'I am not aware of any scientific research anywhere in the world that validates [the assertion that "ecotourism is a very viable alternative to rainforest destruction"]. Local people relationships, rubbish and sewage disposal, firewood sources etc, are all major issues for all jungle lodges which few deal with satisfactorily. Theoretically ecotourism looks good but is rarely in practice and the ecotourism band-wagon is potentially dangerous for many areas and local peoples.'

Certainly the fate of the rainforest and its peoples is a very complex matter, and the relationship between their interests, their governments' and those of the 'developed' world a matter of urgent and often contradictory debate. To anyone interested in reading about the global situation I strongly recommend *In The Rain Forest* by Catherine Caulfield. To anyone interested in the preservation of the 'greatest diversity of wildlife yet discovered in the world', I recommend joining TREES. (Enquiries to John Forrest, 64 Belsize Park, London NW3 4EH.)

naturalists who work there, who can't speak Spanish anyway; so they just see science and naturalism as a gringo thing. It's they who must be made proud of the area they live in.'

A project now in progress close to Explorers, which hoped to rekindle pride in the old customs, language and traditional knowledge of the native Infierno community, was Ametra 2001. It was described in a TREES pamphlet as 'a project set up by Madre de Dios's indigenous people which aims to combine the best of modern and traditional approaches to health-care, in order to maintain acceptable standards of health throughout the region's native forest communities'. Loss of my letter of introduction from Barry the Magus had meant that I had been unable to make the most of a brief, lacklustre meeting in Puerto Maldonaldo with its adviser Didier Lacaze, a slight, diffident Frenchman. I had wanted to spend some time with the Infierno people themselves; but, caught between two worlds, they had a very understandable fear of their traditional knowledge being 'stolen', and did not open up the project to outsiders without good reason.

Crucial modern medicines, David reminded me, like quinine and curare, come from the rainforest and much more potential exists there. In fact, only one per cent of plants in the rainforest have been fully analysed; and yet the forests are being destroyed at the rate of fifty to a hundred acres per minute. Ametra 2001 was engaged in collecting a database of oral knowledge and in persuading local people to rely more on traditional methods rather than, as they saw them, prestigious injections. It was also trying to persuade large drug companies to invest in rainforest protection; investment which would not stem from any sense of altruism on their behalf but because, for the industrialised world, the value of medicines derived from the rainforest runs at over forty billion dollars per year.

'But is one of the main problems,' I asked, 'not that there is intense pressure on land in Peru and that, to the campesinos from the Andes, the rainforest offers some kind of an alternative?'

'Sure,' he said, 'I think to preserve the rainforest it would be better to begin in the Andes. If nothing is done there, the government's saying in effect, "Here's a machete and a matchbox; get on with it." You know, only four per cent of the Andes can be used for intensive agriculture anyway, so the people abandon them to cut rainforest and plant rice. Yet these areas supported far larger populations in Inca times. It is that people are forgetting or just not using Andean technology, so they are exhausting the soil. We need to go back to the old ways: I mean, think of it, it was in the Andes that corn was improved, that the potato was developed. Fourteen million people lived here in Inca times. Fourteen million mouths were fed.'

It was becoming clear to me that agriculture and its problems were a key factor in demographic changes all over Peru. 'Lima is now an Andean city,' Washington Delgado had told me, 'overcrowded with landless campesinos.' Cuzco had seen a similar burgeoning. And from the cities they moved to the forest where their attitudes to the locals were as racist as Limeño attitudes were to them: to the extent that David observed, 'Tropical cultures are disappearing faster than the rainforests themselves.'

David acknowledged the complexity of Peru's problems yet he remained an optimist, becoming most heated when he talked about those who repeated endlessly that Peru was a poor country. 'These people are living outside reality claiming we are poor. We are the richest country in the world in flora and fauna; we have a rich sea and land rich in minerals. We have rainfall, water, soil, food. We are not Ethiopia. We are incapable but we are not poor.'

'Where then does the fault lie?' I asked.

'In people's misconceptions of what progress is about. Listen, I go to places where once there were thousands of alpacas; now I see hundreds of cows and sheep. Alpacas gave wool and meat and their feet do not impact and damage the soil as cows' hooves do. But people decided it was only inferiors who ate alpaca meat. Only cholos. That is an insult for mestizos, what you would call a half-breed. I am a mestizo, a cholo; I have eaten alpaca: the Incas ate alpaca. There is much ignorance and unreality in Peru. Terrorism is an unreality born out of ignorance. The superficial Limeños who think beyond Lima is Miami and Europe, who talk of the 'Indian stain departments' and don't know a campesino is starving – theirs is another unreality. I have realities because I have an education. I have spoken with Sendero, I know how they are thinking. But look,' – David was beginning to spray ideas around the small office in his enthusiasm – 'Peru has a rich sea but no advanced fishing vessel and yet a medium-sized ship can net ten million dollars of fish in one year!'

'You are optimistic then?'

'Yes, I am optimistic. And there are others who realise Peruvians must be more responsible than they are. There is a lot to do and we are the only generation that can do it. For me, we are a rich country. Brazil? What's Brazil got to offer? Sex, a city and a carnival. Peru has so much more. Genetic diversity, the oldest community of life on earth, that is the most important thing Peru has. I'll die happy to know when I was young I was pushing ideas and I was one of the actors saving my country for my grandchildren and all Peruvians.'

¿Qué te parece Peru? – How does Peru appear to you? – was a question I was often asked. The passive construction allowed for the divergent realities David touched on. I was beginning to get a sense that people held too many differing visions of Peru, beyond the often mentioned three realities of costa, selva y cordillera. But I would meet no one whose vision was more noble than David Ricalde's or seen with more clarity: no one who invigorated me more, at a time when I needed it most.

'Everywhere is Robbers!'
ON THE TRUCK TO CHINCHERO

My contact with David had fired me with an interest in Peru again, a desire to engage with it beyond the level of annoyance. Yet after the robbery it was as if everything was in a highlight: the hawkers, the 'comprame, señor' women, the children's shouts of 'cigarros, amigo,' as they trotted beside me, the constant offer of 'dolares, dolares.' I felt my noes were more final; my hand chopped firmly through the air, my head turned away. I was somewhere on the curve of prejudice; aware of an anger I had not dealt with, simmering beneath the surface, showing itself in bad dreams and disgruntled waking.

I had decided against Ecuador: people I had spoken to made it sound cosy, like Switzerland, and there was no easy way from it to Brazil. Instead I would go to Amantani in Lake Titicaca, reputedly a quiet, touristless island, to try to reconstruct what I could of my journal and other writings. 'Worth a go,' Barry had said. 'Sure I believe you can do it.' And true enough, after an afternoon weaving a poem back on to the frayed ends of a loom of broken rhymes, I had leapt up and punched the air with determination. Yeay!

But my spirits in Cuzco this second sojourn in the city had been mercurial to say the least. Now I wanted to do something positive before I left. That was to be a visit to Chinchero market on my final day. I had been told Chinchero was a traditional Andean market and I was interested to see the campesino culture at its most effective.

Early on a Sunday morning I walked up Plateros and then through the narrow streets to where I had been told a bus, colectivo – *some* form of transport – would leave. There was the now familiar feeling of not-a-lot-happening. Campesinos sat around like boulders with their bundles (smaller boulders) beside them. Dogs nosed around in piles of refuse. I kicked my heels and ran my eye along the ruff of mountains surrounding Cuzco, like a tongue over broken teeth.

An obvious gringo approached. He was tall and thin, with a pink, peeling nose and a couple of days' stubble. His hands rested on the small daysack he carried on his chest.

'Per-don-em-e,' he enunciated. '¿Es por el bus por Chinchero?'

'I hope so.'

'Christ, you're not Scottish are you?'

'Aye.'

'Where from?'

'Edinburgh – originally.'

'Me too. Goldenacre. What part you from?'

'Craigleith.'

'Christ – just up the road. You're only the second Scot I've met in ten months.'

'You're the first I've met so far.' And I had almost forgotten the lilt of a Scottish accent, the sense of pleasure that can flow behind its reserve.

A high sided truck arrived. 'Chinchero?' a campesino asked and waved us on. A Norwegian lifted a small Japanese girl on and we followed. As the truck filled we leant over the side and talked about our trips. Ian had been travelling down from the States and through Mexico. I told him about my robbery.

'Oh God, that must be dreadful to lose all that work, all that effort. I've just been lucky so far, touch wood. But you're just waiting for it to happen.' I told him how uneasy I had become when I was approached or touched by anyone. 'Yes, I know. You've got to be so careful.'

A big, broad-shouldered man pushed between us to shout to someone on the street, gesturing at him with a huge banana. 'Hey, hey. Watch your pockets,' we both said in unison and moved back to give the man space.

Ian had a decision coming up: whether to fly home from Miami or to get illegal work in the States and travel some more: 'I really want to see Alaska.' We talked about that moment when travel became a substitute for work (. . . get up in the morning . . . find the train times . . . see the cathedral . . .); for life itself.

'Hang on,' Ian broke in, 'what's going on here?' People were climbing down from the truck and seemed to be forming another queue. When the truck was almost empty, a campesino pointed to my trousers. Running the length of my zipped, 'safe' side pocket was a neat slash: its placing and its length perfect for its purpose.

A few wispy threads stood out. Doubting Thomas, I stared for a couple of seconds before plunging my hand in. Two hundred dollars in American Express traveller's cheques missing, their numbers in my stolen bag.

'Her too,' the Norwegian said and the Japanese held up a small woven bag with a slash down its centre. 'He is in on it,' the Norwegian said, pointing to the stocky driver's mate. 'He gave the man the knife. I saw it.'

And yes, I suddenly recollected the image of the small shining triangle of a Stanley blade being passed out of the driver's cabin: an image that had only momentarily concerned me. Now old and new furies possessed me and I had the man by the neck of his jersey and pushed up against the wall.

'¡Mi dinero, hombre! ¡Mi dinero! Come on, where is it? You were seen! We saw you!' He shook his head as much as I would allow him to. My Spanish cracked in the strain and I unleashed a torrent of verbal abuse whose tone he could not mistake. He was walking off when I reached out, grabbed him again and slapped him across the head.

A campesina spoke up, saying she too had seen him hand over the knife. '¿Policia?' someone suggested.

'Oh, Christ, what can they do?' said bitter experience. But my frustration needed some channel. The small accomplice waved us into the lorry. The driver would take us to the police. 'You've got to be kidding, pal. We'll walk.'

We started off down the hill towards the police station; the culprit, as we saw him, leading the four gringos. At the market he started off down one of the narrow, clothes-thick alleyways, but we pulled him back and shielded him from the warren of stalls.

At the police station we explained the situation to a policeman on guard. The small man made his case and showed his ID. The policeman turned to us: 'Well, none of the robbers carry identification and he does.'

'But we all saw him hand the knife over.' I spoke for us with blinding certainty.

We were led into a room, bare but for a desk, a chair, a row of helmets and a set of bulletproof vests hanging on the wall like carcasses. The case was turned over to another policeman with a mean, bony face and narrow eyes. He slapped the conductor hard over the head for the bother he was causing and on a scrap of paper laboriously took down my name, age, passport number and nationality. He paused after each question, stared over our heads, then jerked out the next as if reading from a cueboard behind us.

El Capitan came in, relaxed in an open-necked white shirt. Neatly groomed, he had gently waved black hair and a trim moustache; the roughness of a bad acne experience on his cheeks.

'Oh, we have so many robbers here,' he started sympathetically, 'and once the money is taken, I'm afraid it's gone.' He turned to the small conductor who stood silently in the corner clutching his crumpled wad of fares. El Capitan had a baton in his hand now and was winding its strap around his wrist. 'Who were the others, eh?' he hissed. We had deduced there must have been at least four: himself, the big, distracting man and two women, one of whom had the incisive skill of a surgeon. But it could have been that the whole truck was a set-up: corral the gringos then fleece them. And the evidence we had to offer? One of them was carrying the biggest banana you've ever seen!

El Capitan poked the baton hard into the small man's stomach, doubling him, then raised it as if he was going to bring it down on his curled shoulder. It stayed poised there for a moment and another question, another proclamation of innocence, then he brought it down ready to drive into the small man's stomach again.

Initially, the openness of the violence, the supposedly shared assumptions behind it, had shocked us. We looked at each other wide-eyed, confused by an alien etiquette, and for a moment I was lost somewhere between memories of Samaná and Graham Greeneland. When I got my breath back I pushed between them.

'Please, señor, it's my two hundred dollars that's been stolen but I don't want this. Please.'

In one movement el Capitan swivelled round and sat on the edge of the table, all sympathy and charm, as if there had been no smudging between the polite and the brutal: Jekyll and Hyde, the line was easily crossed.

'We have so many robbers here,' he repeated, 'so many. And you're leaving tomorrow. We really need to go round markets and houses and you can say, "Is this the thief?" But it takes so much time and you're leaving tomorrow. Ay-ay-ay. You must take great care. Great care. You put your money here' – he indicated a side pocket – 'they slash it. You must put your money here,' and he grabbed two handfuls of his crotch.

'I don't know,' I said, 'I'd rather be slashed *here*, than *there*!'

Everyone laughed, but for the ashen-faced small man in the shadows, in his ragged, striped jersey and his cheap trainers with his mop of black hair and his patchy moustache which would never meet in the middle.

'No, but really,' el Capitan repeated, 'you must take care.' I wondered aloud whether it was possible to buy one of their bulletproof vests and whether there were trousers to match; but really I wanted to be away from this place where even my pure anger had been stolen from me.

'What's to happen to him?' I asked.

'Oh, he'll stay here.'

'Well, listen, it's my two hundred dollars,' I repeated, 'and I don't want him beaten.'

'Sure, sure, sure.'

'Eh, *gracias*, eh, señor,' I half spat at the small man as I turned my back on him and left.

I entered the Tourist Police at the head of the four of us in a mood for answers. Later a gringo who was in the chief's office described me as behaving 'like a demented Scotsman.' I felt I had good cause.

I asked first about my bag and felt my breathing quicken when the chief seemed unable to find my deposition. Eventually he pulled it from a pile of papers. Nothing. Nothing other than an obvious desire to be rid of me. But I had prepared my questions: How often does this happen? Why were there no policemen on the airport floor? Why is there no advice given at the tourist office about avoiding robberies? Why do I have to buy a certificate from the Banco de la Nacion to register my loss?

Ignominiously, I was hustled out after my second question clutching my scrap of question paper. In answer to the first the chief told me they were not allowed to divulge such information: it was classified. Later one of the gringos in the office told me that in the book of depositions, which began at the end of January, they were already (in the second week of April) at page 152, with three entries per double page. The second question he rejected out of hand, and that was that.

Four gringos sat in a row in the chief's office with the dejected look of the recently robbed. One girl shouted out to me as I was bundled out that she had lost her camera and money. A New Zealander pointed to a grey pair of Rohans slit exactly like mine had been. Bulging with petty rancour I pushed my way back in the door to shout to them, 'There's a poster out here. Know what it says? "Peru es todo – y algo." Peru is everything and something more. Well, we all know what the *something more* is, don't we?'

Even the policeman at the desk laughed with us.

On the street again, suddenly I felt I was in the middle of a farce – 'POLICE SEARCH FOR THE BIG BANANA IS ON – and the discovery that actually I did have my cheque numbers in my moneybelt and that it was the photocopies that had been stolen made me almost light-headed. With the most impressive efficiency and a phone call to Tucson, the American Express Office in Avenida del Sol issued me with a fresh set after half an hour's verification: necessary, Ian told me, because there are so many freeloaders who keep on going by selling their cheques and claiming they have been stolen.

We carried on down Avenida del Sol to Radio Tawantinsuyo where, on last-minute *South American Handbook* advice, I placed ten radio adverts for my notebooks. I noted the *Handbook* clearly stated that you were not to expect the police to break into a sweat over your losses. So there was nothing else to do then but head for the Vareyoc Café and try to relax. I had done much of my writing and rewriting of poems there. The atmosphere was of a calm Edinburgh café: classical music played softly; Peruvian newspapers were available. It was my *Not Peru*. I had also been having problems with my gut. Though there were tasty meals to be had in Peru – seafood and chifa (Chinese) – often poor quality or bland ingredients were disguised by chili, herbs and strong seasoning. As a cuisine it was not very attractive to the man who had left half his insides across Central Asia two years before. But the Vareyoc offered fresh coffee and slices of pizza and harmless empanadas, meat or cheese-filled pasties, which were friendly to all tummies.

As a cheese and tomato pizza was put before Ian and me, the four gringos from the tourist police office came in. We gathered round a large table to discuss our losses.

They had also been robbed around the Chinchero 'bus stop'. One English girl had fallen a few yards behind her companions and, as thirty spectators looked on, lost her daysack, with its camera, cash and diary, in a tug-of-war with the thief. The New Zealander had kicked off two robbery attempts, catching one man in the face, before his trousers were finally slashed in a similar way to mine.

'It's a bloody national industry.'

'They're like magicians.'

'Sometimes you can buy your camera back in Puno or La Paz, the *Handbook* says.'

'Yea, but not to get wild with the guy selling it because he might have had nothing to do with the theft.'

'They probably make you pay more for it because it's of sentimental value.'

A Frenchman, who had arrived on the scene just too late to save the English girl's bag, pointed to an advert in a colour supplement for a company called grupo 4: *SEGURIDAD INTEGRAL . . . en MANOS PERUANOS* (Complete security in Peruvian hands.)

Humour was our unreality. For although much was laughable, much was also very worrying. As Ian said, 'After one robbery, you've got to prepare immediately for the next.' And how would that come about? With another distraction? Spit down the back, an epileptic fit, a jostling. Keep your ears open. In Trujillo they practise 'the live rat trick'. At traffic lights they throw a live rat on to the lap of a woman driver. Usually the car is soon theirs. Vigilance always. But then you hear a traveller at the railway station, prepared as a medieval knight, daysack on his front, chickenwire behind, was hit by five fat women, coming at him from all directions. On his back like a beetle, three sat on him while two ripped his daysack from his chest.

'Lima Airport. A policeman told me I should pay a policeman to escort me to a taxi.'

'Taxis – huh. I heard of one guy, he's just arrived, gets in this taxi. The driver turns the engine over a couple of times; says, "What it needs is a little push."'

'Oh no, he doesn't, does he?'

'Yeah, out he gets, pushes and of course it's the last he sees of his stuff.'

'You're going to Brazil? Well, we were in Brazil for six weeks; four robbery attempts. How long you going for?'

I did not want to think about that yet. The next day I was to take the train to Puno, yet another notorious journey.

'What you've got to watch is that for about two hours there are no lights in the train.'

'No lights!'

'Yes. And they reckon it's because the train drivers are in league with the robbers. Like some of the bus drivers are.'

The next day also, Ian would take the bus to Lima which skirted Sendero territory. He was not particularly looking forward to it. 'When I was coming to Peru, that's what someone said: "The jungle's drugs, the mountains are terrorists and the coast's robbers." '

'Oh no,' said the Frenchman with feeling, 'I think everywhere is robbers!'

Back in Hostal America I smiled wanly at the owner as I pointed to my ripped trousers. I went to my room and calmed myself with some invisible mending. Then, as another kind of exorcism, I made up a list of:

GRINGO NIGHTMARES

1 The countries are doubling.
2 The dollar is falling.
3 You're down to your last two imodium.
4 All the shoeshiners you've said 'Mañana' to are waiting for you.
5 'There are those who torture and those who get tortured.' (Graham Greene: *The Power and the Glory*. According to Ian.) Your skin is getting darker. But it's not with the sun.
6 A bundle of rancid meatbones on a packed train.
7 Everyone near you holds a razor in the palm of his hand.
8 You've strayed off the gringo map. Where are you? There are no ruins. There are no mind-blowing landscapes. There is dust, poverty and many natural thieves.
9 You've run out of toilet paper.
10 They're training their children to rob as soon as the little bastards can walk.
11 They're laughing at you.
12 You have forgotten: where was it the terrorism stopped, the drug-running began?
13 Your clothes are all neatly cut to ribbons: you spin like a maypole.
14 You're walking down the road and in each doorway, in each alleyway, they're sizing you up. They're laughing at you.
15 For your life, you must answer truthfully: do you think they're worth as much as you? Though you journey so far to see their ancient endeavours.

16 You were caught by an old trick – the oldest in the book. You are centre-stage in an old music-hall. The place is packed with gringos, all guffawing: 'Oh Lord, not that old chestnut!'
17 You're moving so fast, you're running out of countries . . .

Later that evening, going on my farewell walk round Cuzco, I fought to be positive, talking to myself like a character in a novel I was reading at the time, David Copperfield's aunt. 'We must meet reverses boldly, not suffer them to frighten us, my dear. We must learn to act the play out. We must live misfortune down, Trot.'

I walked down Loreto to Coricancha. It was good to see and touch the Inca stones again; to remind myself of the depth this city had: the dignity beyond the constant assault of the hustlers. I had known a few evenings here when it was chilly and wet – the nights were generally cold – but now it was pleasant; warm as a good summer evening in Scotland. Huge orange and white ascension clouds piled up behind the church of La Compañia. Its stonework and that of the cathedral glowed a warm red in the fading sun.

> Cuzco, Cuzco es tu nombre sagrado
> como el sol del incario inmortal.
> Todo el mundo te lleva en el pecho
> como canto y bandera triunfal.

Looking down the long straight of Avenida del Sol, I saw a rainbow's end brushing the sign dug into the hillside: 'Viva el Peru'.

'Oh God, every day it seems I'm speaking to a mate who's just been robbed,' said Woody, sometime Cross Key's barman, in his thick Lancashire accent. 'It's bloody depressing. I don't know what's happening to this place.' He told me however that two years before he had had his journal stolen and written it out again and that it was better second time around. 'Something about it going through the filtration of memory, I reckon.'

I thanked him for his cheering thought and walked over to interrupt Barry who was involved with a small group of well-heeled tourists at the far end of the bar. I had a parting question for him.

'Shoot, mate.'

'David Ricalde says that to him Manu is Peru. Biological diversity is the most important thing Peru has. It's the basis of his feelings of nationalism.'

'Right. So?'

'So my question is, what's Peru to you?'

'Birds and adventure. There are places here where no white man's ever been. Every day is an adventure.'

'That sounds very egocentric compared to David's thinking. You're saying it's just a place where you're happy.'

'Exactly. You know the last time I went back to Britain, I was going for a month but I changed my flight and left two weeks early. I was bored. All these guys on the Underground from the airport, all pretending the others don't exist. You couldn't get half a dozen Peruvians together without them gabbing away like crazy. So let's just say I'm happy here. I'm not going to philosophise about it. Here though, mate, let me buy you a drink. I mean, I'll never see you again. And listen, be careful on that train. Three places to watch: Sicuani, Juliaca and Puno itself. I tell you, some gringo in your carriage will be robbed.' This last was spoken with Old Testament certitude.

I paid Barry the fifteen dollars we had agreed on for a small, black Andean Equipment daysack to keep my new notebooks in and left him selling jewellery to his tour group. 'No, this is expensive stuff, mate,' he told me. 'Hand-beaten silver with pre-Colombian stones.'

'None of the Worst'
CUZCO TO PUNO

I slept poorly, dreaming of circuses and fairs; packed places, like David Copperfield's London, where fear and deceit were bred. 'My aunt had . . . this other general opinion . . . that every man she saw was a pick-pocket.'

My mind played over my first robbery. The man's face was indistinct, a tall mestizo with large, softly frowning features, but I still heard his voice clearly: 'Sucio.' Said only the once, but in memory so deep I could analyse each syllable. '*Su-ci-o.*' Said slowly, but now I realised like someone acting concern – the first syllable went amateurishly low – not genuinely shocked and disgusted. I heard the fat man who had a room beneath me retching violently to spit his all. I imagined he was filling a plastic screw-top, getting ready for 'work'.

My thoughts rippled out to the airport, then to the bus to Chinchero, to the large numbers of people who were there, who must have seen what was going on, who did nothing. Was this tacit cooperation? Acceptance? Approval? Or just the lethargy of the snake? Was it part of David Ricalde's we-are-poor-therefore unreality? And the official bodies themselves seemed to ignore the reality of all these robberies. At the tourist office I had asked, 'Where do I get the bus to Chinchero?'

'Arcopata.' And the woman put a neat cross at the spot. No mention of, 'But be careful, it's a notorious place for set-ups, for bag-snatches, for trouser-slashing.' And no policemen in sight.

In the darkness I had an image of the loss of my writing. It had to do with height and space. As I wrote my journal I had felt the thickness of the left-hand side grow pleasantly fat – a satisfying fertility. I mounted the steps of each morning with a neat day and date. And then suddenly, it was gone. It was like diving into a huge space, a timeless space. The past – where was it? The future – what

91

was the point? It was a feeling almost of free-falling light-headedness.
I was falling, falling, shouting louder, louder:

Soy escritor

Soy escritor

Soy ESCRITOR.

I had never really felt it before or known what it meant. Usually
I looked sheepish – it is the custom in Scotland – and claimed 'to
write a bit'. Now, now that all was lost, lost too was the vanity of
the bulging notebook, the diversity of material, the forward-looking
pleasure of unpacking my treasures and giving them some kind of
independent life. And all that was left was this bloodied, raw desire
to write; to acknowledge 'this also happened; this also will be written
about.' I saw in my eyes not just the trace of a hunted look, but a
determination: '*Soy escritor.*' Some things you cannot steal. For five
hours I had thought about and written about Machu Picchu at the
highest level of my consciousness. And certain kinds of knowledge
you can only find out one way – through pain. In this, loving and
writing, I discovered, are similar pursuits.

> If your love was true
> and you lose it, what have you lost?
> Not the act of loving. That's yours.
>
> If your words were true
> and you lose them, what have you lost?
> Not the act of writing. That's yours too.
>
> In loving, in writing, how can you
> hold on to a finished thing? Whether
> you lose it or put it beneath glass,
>
> it is the act itself you must cherish.
> For what's left when the moment has passed,
> the wind will carry. Despite you.

Before I set off for the station for the train to Puno, I loaded up with
imodium to seal my loose, nervous bowels; folded my chain and felt
its weight in my hand. There was no way I wanted to be robbed again
and I determined if I had to stand in a queue it would be with this
chain in my hand. I took deep breaths and felt for my moneybelt and
the stiffness of traveller's cheques secreted about me. I thought of the

fearful apprehension of the drug smuggler at the start of *Midnight Express*, his heart thumping, beads of guilty sweat on his lips.

I paid the hostel owner three thousand intis for the last time and he handed me the neat slip, carefully signed and stamped twice: 'Hostal America PAGADO.' I shook his hand, before stepping out into the street.

It had been a strange place, Hostal America. Situated only fifty metres up Plateros from the Plaza de Armas, it was central and quiet, yet unpopular with most gringo tourists: its staple was a thin trickle of Peruvians who had come to Cuzco for work. Although a spacious courtyard made the small rooms light, and I was well served by a bed, table and chair of Van Gogh simplicity, I could not deny that an air of melancholy hung over the place. The owner, a bachelor in his fifties, slept on a camp-bed in the vestibule of the hostel and cooked on a two ring stove in the courtyard, mostly a kind of vegetable stew as far as I could make out. Every morning I heard the tinny radio play as he washed, hung up and ironed sheets. One afternoon I had seen him painfully sewing on a shirt-button. The outside door was always chained and, when I had rung from outside or inside the hostel, I would hear his shuffling, forward-leaning run, his muted 'Buenas.'

His help on the other hand had been a short, rude young man with a baseball cap glued to his head, whose greetings always verged on the cheaply insulting: 'Hey-hey-hey! *Bue-nas*.' I was sure he had had a gloating look in his eyes when he found out I had been robbed. But then I was riding the curve of prejudice.

I arrived at the station in good time and chained my travel-bag to the luggage rack. It was turning into a bright, sunny morning. I had a window seat. Breathing deeply, I told myself: 'Relax.'

The carriage filled up. My space was shared with a girl going to Juliaca, holding a large cardboard box on her lap, and a young family of campesinos. The mother of the two children, a toddler and a baby, could not have been more than twenty. The husband was drunk. I had seen his arm around the weeping mother he was leaving. His eyes were hooded and white spittle had formed at the corners of his mouth. He leaned over the breastfeeding baby, giggling inanely. Occasionally I heard 'el gringo', followed by some mumbled comment and a laugh. *Relax*, I told myself again; but was relieved when finally he slumped over into sleep.

I came to know the mother's breasts well. She left one out as both she and the baby dozed; or she placed the baby on the table and lifted a breast to its mouth. It was impressive how she coped with the two children for the twelve hours to Juliaca while her boorish husband slept, the baby's shawl across his face. Like most of the Peruvian children I had seen, the toddler appeared self-sufficient already. She made few demands on her parents but sat quietly, playing with an orange in a plastic mug. A quarter of Peruvian children die before their first birthday and those who survived, it seemed, learned early not to expect anything; there were never any toys. Though she had the liquid brown eyes, the shiny black hair of a child, already this toddler had the little rough hands of a campesina.

The landscape changed from the lushness of the Urubamba valley into the sweeping emptiness of bare hills, the sky holding the rare fleck of a red-backed hawk or the huge wingspan of the black-chested buzzard eagle. The train chugged down to the mountain-ringed plains where sheep and alpaca were herded by bowler-hatted women. Every so often a mongrel dog would run from a mud-brick farmhouse and race the train furiously. What improbable thoughts could they have been having?

The track was like a river bringing life, custom and commerce. At the bigger settlements small groups of 'merchants' squatted along the track selling everything from sheep's heads, staring blindly on the blanket before them, to rusting automobile parts.

All around the region of Lake Titicaca the women traditionally top colourful costumes of billowing skirts and woollen jerseys with bowler hats. I thought of the corruption of the North American Indians' dress and the sullen dejection Robert Louis Stevenson had observed in the ragged groups of defeated Indians which gathered around his train as it moved through the Great Plains.

This train – every train! – was so packed you would think there was no way through the carriage, but a constant stream of vendors, women and boys mostly, moved through between stations, dipping and ducking, squeezing past passengers.

'¡Chicles! ¡Chicles! ¡Chicles!'
'¡Chocolate! ¡Cigarrillos!'
'¡Ceramicas!'
'¡Patatas rellenas!'
'¡Gaseosas!'

The women entered with great baskets on their shoulders. They pulled away brown paper to reveal chunks of roasted lamb or ribs or potatoes stuffed with spicy rice. Portions were given in scraps of paper and eaten with the fingers, the locals expertly peeling a boiled potato like a squirrel with a nut. But through it all, the forbearance, stoicism and good humour of the Peruvians was again impressive. Some of them stood uncomplainingly for ten hours, only shoving a bundle past them a little more forcefully than necessary. I could not imagine such sweet temper if the Edinburgh to London train had been similarly jammed, or *pace* Roland, the Frankfurt to Cologne.

Still, it was not only the thick smells of fat and spices, making me clench my buttocks, which dulled my enjoyment of this journey. I had felt for the first time a gnawing loneliness, finding echoes of familiar landscapes in the sweep of a glen, the gentle bend of a river. I was thinking it would be nice to spend some time travelling with someone else, to share the strain but, as we entered the darkness which had me constantly glancing up to check the shadow of my bag, my only companion was the bearded, dark-eyed twin who stared back at me from the occluded window.

The tracks split Juliaca like a western cow town. I had noted that the *Handbook* called Juliaca 'lawless'. But, with its dimly lit rows of mud and brick house-huts and deeply rutted mud roads, it looked more abandoned than free. Just before we arrived at the station, the lights came on. People gathered their belongings, my 'companions' among them, and most of the train emptied.

I stood up to stretch my legs, to rub my put-upon bum, when suddenly there was an eruption at one end of the carriage and an American shouted, 'Hey, watch it! They tried to set us up!' And three men hurried through the carriage before an American woman's shout, 'They got my bag! They got my bag! Everything! They got everything!'

My heart sinks and the lights go out: the carriage doors are mysteriously locked. 'Some gringo in your carriage will be robbed.'

A Swedish couple and a German guy sitting near me were on their feet, that sickened expression on their faces too. The Frenchman from the tourist police the day before had been sitting opposite the victims. He called to me, 'Hey, watch your stuff, eh! Here, there's space. Come and join us.' I unchained my bag and did so.

I remembered the overweight, middle-aged American couple

when they boarded the train; both carried green backpacks on
their chests and had what looked like an assortment of small army
hold-alls on a belt around their waists. Easy meat. It turned out the
travel agent had told them their tickets were for tourist class where
they would be safe. But they had been issued with first class tickets.
Tourist class: 30,000 intis. First class: 5,800 intis. 'Everywhere is
robbers.' A tall French-Canadian and a Japanese-American girl who
sat with them had taken the precaution of handing their luggage
over to someone in tourist class where the doors were locked for the
duration of the journey.

How it happened. Five guys. Two talk to the couple, offering
them special hotel deals etc. The other two crowd round while the
fifth crawls or reaches beneath the seat and grabs the bag.

'I told them,' Bernard whispered to me, 'tie your bags up on the
rack but they wouldn't listen.' Bernard was on a round the world
trip and he had a system worked out for the South American leg
that seemed to be based on the storming of Himalayan peaks. He
had a large backpack with him but he was going back to La Paz:
he had left another bag and more valuables there while he made
his assault on Cuzco. He would then take these on to Lima to leave
with a friend for the next stage of his journey. He had photocopies
of everything everywhere. Still, he was not optimistic. 'So far I am
lucky, but I know sometime it will happen.' With his long face
and straw-coloured hair pulled back in a half-hearted ponytail, he
reminded me of a youthful Donald Sutherland; the same doomy
seriousness suddenly lightened by a wry humour.

What the lady had lost were clothes and make-up. I told her to
make up a list of the contents now for her deposition the next day
as I had forgotten to mention much of what was in my bag. I told
again how it had happened to me, and the trouser-slashing too. 'Tell
as many people as you can how it happened,' Barry had said. And I
did so: the Ancient Mariner but without his enthusiasm, knowing
that my story would spread out in waves, carried by travellers inside
and outside South America.

'And there was this one guy and he was a writer and he lost . . .'

'Wow, how dreadful. I wouldn't mind losing my stuff but I'd hate
to lose my films. I mean, they're memories.' And in my mind I saw
them reaching between their legs to clutch their precious bags.

As a dim, brown light from Juliaca station filtered through the
carriage, a league table of the most dangerous Latin American

countries was drawn up. It went: Colombia ('It's worse there, they don't do tricks, just knife you and rob you.'), Peru ('Machu Picchu, Okay. But lots of people aren't even risking that, just flying over the whole mess.') and Brazil.

The sandy-haired, handsome French-Canadian, Gilles, worked as a tour guide in Rio. Now standing commandingly in the aisle, he delighted in telling stories about the city. 'Rio is big, it's fast and it's dangerous.' But he knew where to go, where to avoid and nothing had happened to him. He had plenty of tales of what had happened to others, though; the most gruesome being a double-headed story about an American tourist who had refused to pay a taxi driver's extortionate rates. 'He put down the money that had been initially agreed upon. The taxi driver waited until he was twenty yards away and then shot him. Both legs. It's happened twice this year.' As if it was something only experience could teach, he advised, 'If they have a gun or a knife, whatever you've got, hand it over. It's not worth dying or having a slashed face.'

The American woman had tabulated the contents of her sack at four hundred and fifty dollars.

'Well, clothes are cheap here anyway,' said Gilles.

'Yeah,' she drawled, 'but I'm sized about twice what these local women are.'

Ten minutes after the robbery, the lights came on.

When the train reached Puno we left it as if on a military exercise. 'Watch, don't get too close to those in front. Make space.'

'Watch those three guys with the limping one in the middle. Could be a set-up.'

It was raining and it was threatening. Bernard and I took a taxi to a hostel. A German tourist we met there, who had come tourist class from Cuzco, told us how she had given money and pens at each stop to the children who crowded the carriage windows. 'I don't like doing it,' she said, 'but I don't like not doing it.' Whether you beg from the gringo or steal from him, he can afford it, eh? I remembered some graffiti scratched on the inside of a toilet door in the medina at Fez: 'This is the only place they can't get your dirams from you.'

In the morning Bernard went off to La Paz. I gave him the wish I had decided was most appropriate for South America.

'Hey, Bernard, none of the worst, eh.'

'None of the worst.'

I went to change money, then strolled down to the small port to talk to the boat owners about getting to Amantani. It was a relief to be out of Cuzco. Compared to that city, Puno had the improvised feel of a settlement. There was nothing to do, or demanding to be done, but hang around; to visit the market where gringos stoked up on alpaca jerseys much cheaper than in Cuzco. I felt my shoulders relax a little, thinking of the tranquil week ahead.

I met Gilles holding court with some fresh tourists in a café. An Israeli couple were going to Cuzco then flying to Lima. I warned them about the airport.

'How did it happen?'

I sketched the details.

'Oh, that one. I found out about that in Buenos Aires.'

'Yea, they do it in Rio too. It's in the *Handbook*.'

'You've got to wrap the strap around your foot.'

I thought to myself, they would have razored that easily; but I suddenly felt inadequate. I remembered our family friend chalk-haired Auntie Irene, Great World Traveller, whose suitcase had been slashed in Cuzco, looking up at me and saying, 'Oh, but they won't try anything with you. The size of you! You'd just give them a real good biff.' I had obviously forgiven myself far too easily; and saying to myself I had gained from the loss in any way was just pure sophistry. It was like revisiting that horrible first sinking feeling. The talk had moved on to Brazil's thieves, particularly Rio's, leaving me feeling vulnerable again – like a man with one leg.

I went to the busy market with Gilles to buy fruit and candles for Amantani. Being robbed is losing the confident skin you have grown naturally; it is to know it can happen to you and if it has happened once . . .

The non-robbed make more relaxing if complacent company and Gilles, big loudmouth that he was, gave out an air of confidence that was appealing to me at the time. Also, he had given me his number in Rio. 'Call me, eh. It's a big city; you've got to know what you're doing. But you've got a friend there now.'

I did phone him when I got to Rio a couple of months later. His wife answered and I heard a background conversation before she came back to the phone. 'You the Scottish guy, right? Leave your number and Gilles will call you.' I knew he would not but I was not too disappointed. I had got over my nerves by then (was even thinking *Travels With My Angst* might not be the most suitable title for my book) and was able to take a more even view of the handsome tour guide who had confessed to me, 'This has been a good trip for me. Three things I've always wanted to do: go to Machu Picchu, put my foot in Lake Titicaca and make it with an oriental chick. And this trip I've done all three. You've seen my little Japanese, yeah? Not bad, yeah? Yeah? And she's a lively little thing too.'

That night, sleep once again eluded me. Dogs barked in the cold, thin air. One started a base line *ruff* . . . *ruff* . . . *ruff* . . . Another overlaid that with a more improvisory *woof-woof* . . . *woof-woof-woof* . . . More joined in. Like a camera my restless mind followed the rabid mongrels of Puno as they roamed down the narrow streets, through the tight patchwork of market stalls, over the rubble-lined railway track, to fight at last over a pair of cow's horns I had seen earlier topping a pile of refuse. Still joined, the central bone was spotted with gristle and blood.

Adrift at Last
AMANTANI

I

It was a three-hour ride to Amantani in a small, partially covered boat across Lake Titicaca: one hundred and thirty miles long by forty-one miles wide; at 3,812 metres the highest navigable water in the world. I had bought my one-way ticket from an agency near the harbour for five thousand intis (roughly three dollars at that time). A serious American tourist had bought his round trip ticket from an agency in the centre of Puno and had paid twenty-eight thousand intis. ('Everywhere there is robbers.') 'I don't mind,' he mumbled unconvincingly, 'I've only got two weeks' vacation. Don' wanna waste it haggling.'

Of course Lake Titicaca is renowned for more than impressive statistics and a name like a birdcall. For it was from its icy blue waters that the first Sun Emperor Manco Capac and his sister-wife emerged – one legend has it they came from the Island of the Sun, now in Bolivian waters. Manco Capac carried with him a golden staff. Wherever it sank, there they would found a new kingdom. They journeyed through the Andes, the rocky landscape repelling the staff until it sank in a valley in the centre of the earth. This was to be the site of Cuzco. However, centuries before this mythical event, the Tiahuanuco culture had swept across Peru, earning Lake Titicaca its historical reputation as 'the cradle of Andean civilisation'.

Our boat took a short stop-over at one of the unlikely floating islands of Uros. These islands, of which there are about forty, are made out of layers of tortora reeds, and each year the islanders must add fresh straw as the floor is tramped down and the bottom of the island rots.

Simple tent-shaped straw huts stood on the spongy surface with fish-tails at their doorways and rumpled blankets inside. Pigs rooted about the matted floor. Women offered tapestries and models of the moon-shaped canoes moored there, made out of tightly bound bundles of reeds.

Three to four hundred Indians, most of them Catholics, now live like this on the scatter of islands. When the Incas controlled this area, I was told by *The Rough Guide to Peru* (my chattier, more colourful back-up to the 'bible'), 'they considered the Uros so poor – almost sub-human – that only a section of hollow cane filled with lice was required from them as a monthly tribute.' I doubted they could afford much more today, but the small dirty children seemed happy enough on their thirty by twenty yards of straw. A cynic among us suggested the people were brought out in the early morning for the tourists to snap their unlikely habitat. Whatever the arrangement, neither side let the other down. Give. Give. Give. Snap. Snap. Snap.

And again snap. Yet when Luzma, my sympathetic travel agent, took me in a taxi down to contrabando in Cuzco, it had not been to buy a camera. I had needed to replace my torch, nicked in Nazca, and my alarm.

'Bring nothing with you,' she had advised and, laughing uproariously, told me to keep the taxi window up. This was Peru as farce. 'They just reach in and snatch,' she squealed. 'What a place!'

The market had been dense as a souk, tables heaved with cameras, yet I had not been tempted. For long before my camera had been stolen I had noticed the unhealthy reliance people had on photographs, and their ability to take them, to make sense of what they saw. What was a suitable response to beauty? 'The Valley of the Moon was really good. I shot a whole thirty-six in an hour. That's how good it was.' A suitable response to grandeur? 'Machu Picchu? I took about four rolls. Beauties.' Or to poverty? The same. It precluded any necessity to make sense of something yourself, to make real connections. For me, not having one was strangely liberating and concentrating: there was no way I could postpone the moment.

Still, sometimes when I saw a camera lifted to a scene I would like to have shared back home, I felt a twinge of loss and was suddenly conscious of my idle hands, like someone who has recently given up smoking. Out of interest and this bitter loss, I had even started to collect snippets of 'Camera Stories' instead. Like this conversation I overheard on Uros.

ENGLISH GIRL (walking around the island as if she's lost something important): I left my camera in Ecuador. I just didn't want to risk it. But there are times like now when I really miss it.

AMERICAN (whose girlfriend is furiously snapping): Yeah, know what you mean. After we lost our camera we could have bought another one at the market, but we thought they were over-priced. So what happened? We spent the most exciting six weeks of our lives without a fucking camera because we didn't want to spend eighty dollars.

Fade on two heads, shaking.

The island of Uros we visited lay in the middle of the sheltered Gulf of Chucuito. The rooted islands of Amantani and Taquile lay beyond it, like guardians, one at each side of its neck. A Californian with a thick blond pelt, face daubed with sunblock and a group leader complex whooped away the silence on the roof of the boat. But the sun's rays reflected wickedly off the intense blue waters of the lake, so it was from the small window of the launch that I – a different creature by far – watched the pyramid shape of Taquile drift by, and the few kilometres of Amantani come into view.

From the approach Amantani looked barren, rocky and sparsely inhabited. I wondered if this had been the right place to come at all. From our mooring at the pier, panting in the heat, we walked up a long steep, straight track, which led to the main village where accommodation in private houses was to be allocated; there were no hotels or pensiones. The *Handbook* suggested a Ricardo Quispe Mamani who also had a small restaurant on the main square. His heavily built wife showed me my room and soon I was on the end of a bench in the small dark restaurant, supping soup with the few day-trippers; listening to their stories.

'There was a field of women working and I thought, that'll make a good photograph,' the camera-bereft girl began. 'I climbed down the banking and took this photograph. All of a sudden this woman downs her hoe and runs up to me demanding money. Well, I don't have anything on me, so she grabs my sunglasses and races away across the field. She wasn't young either. Anyway, gallant Chris comes down and rescues my sunglasses. It ends up they stone him as he walks away.' Snap!

The next day I would take a brand-new notebook from my bag. It measured six inches by four and was three quarters of an inch thick, with thread-bound pages. I would open its black and white marbled cover and, beneath my name and address, write 'Amantani, 12 April 1989' and then, as neatly as possible, the plagiarism, deeply felt, 'SPEAK MEMORY'.

And to ease my memory, to free from it some of the words, the phrases I had already written – precious seeds – I would walk and walk; walk like a man without a camera, who only has his diary to record what he sees.

II

I am standing with Joe, a round the world Australian, beneath eucalyptus trees, looking over a landscape that can be read like a Breughel. ('If you can just get me between these trees with the mountains in the background. Oh yes, that's one for the wall!') Neat fields slope down to the still water. A woman bent with a bundle of vegetables passes along a stony path. A young girl skips down the steep path with a small sack of potatoes. There is a slurp in the silence, as a man digs with a hand-plough. The sharp smell of the eucalyptus surrounds us.

'Well, I've only got one thing to say to you,' says Joe, as I wave him and the other day-trippers off: 'Lucky bastard!'

I walk round the rocky coast, clambering over many walls, and am baited by three small boys. They go off whistling when it is obvious I'm not going to give them anything. Something in me still revolts at an outright demand: it draws me into explanations of the connection between money and work. Calvinist dullard! The boys agree. With the catapults they use to keep birds from the crops, they launch a couple of parting stones far over my head.

I climb up to my room from the small courtyard by a steep wooden ladder and stoop through the doorway, as I must through all the doorways here. The room is about ten feet by twelve with pink adobe walls and a buckled floor. Three small windows – and the door left open – make the room light. If I squint at one window, I look over the plaza. Somehow on this rich, fertile island, a centrepiece has been contrived of dull concrete. Four sparse squares of grass surround a clumsy stone plinth with the incongruous bust of Miguel Grau, a seriously mutton-chopped Peruvian hero, sitting sternly on top. On two sides of the square are houses of mud-brick and concrete; on the other two the barn of a church with its squat, square bell-tower and the municipal building. Any sense of proportion these two buildings may have had has been ruined by the crudest crazy-paving kind of plasterwork.

The other two windows look over the thatched roof of the kitchen hut to a stand of eucalyptus trees, the waters of the lake and the mainland peninsula of Capachica.

The room is furnished with two iron beds, a shaky table and a stone stool that Roberto, the thirteen-year-old son, has dragged in for me.

The sun has just gone down. I sit in my room by candlelight, the distant black silhouettes of land through the window strangely calming. I am adrift at last.

I hear steps up the wooden ladder. It is Juanita, the girl, with baby Sophia on her back. I noticed her hanging around the bar, staring through its window, while I ate my fish and potatoes. Claris, the toddler, comes in soon after her.

Juanita smiles shyly: 'She is heavy,' and nods her head backwards. Claris looks out from under her limp-brimmed woollen hat and asks me for an orange with a charming broken-toothed smile. I give her one and they stay watching me – which I gather, in the absence of any attempt at conversation, is the point of their visit – as I write. 'Muy bueno,' says Juanita before she leaves.

When the last shouts of the kick and chase footballers have died, Roberto arrives. He too leans beside me, watching me write. He flicks through an edge of the notebook. 'Hay mucho.' It pleases me to hear it. 'Come on, Roberto, I'll buy you a Coke.'

I drink a beer as the family move around me, smiling. Then at eight o'clock, the señora says, 'Well, shall we go?' Branches are jammed against the doors and we all retire for the night.

In the night a ferocious hail-storm rattles on the tin roof. At six in the morning I hear the children laughing, hear the radio, then the scrunching as they rake and stamp through hail which lies like a covering of snow on the shadowed courtyard. Water drips from the ledges of white hail caught on the straw roofs. Soon, though, smoke is coming out of the straw-stack and hot sun is turning the water into steam.

The English couple and the blond Californian who are staying one night arrive. I walk with them round one point of the island, till we see the pyramid of Taquile. It is very beautiful: the azure water clear and cold. Chris, tall, lithe and manly, strips off and goes in for a swim in his panda-briefs. Two boys arrive after spotting us in the distance. They pull toy boats made out of old soya bean oil cans. *Pico Flor* one boat is called; *San José* the other. I give them lollipops, so they perform enthusiastically, showing us the speed of their boats as they skiff them through the water and how many stones they can carry before sinking. When they decide to go for a swim there's a real rigmarole because of the presence of the English girl. Eventually they take a plastic sack they've found on the beach, drape it round the pair of them and walk into the water, giggling. It's soon forgotten though, as is their nakedness. I think of Frank Meadow Sutcliffe's 'Water Sprites', watching them dive badly and execute impressively unimpressive water-tricks: slim, brown sprites.

We return to the village by a twisting route over the back of the island. 'Didn't I just know it! Didn't I just know it!' the Californian curses. 'The minute I take that last photograph, ten yards on the view's even more beautiful.'

In the afternoon there's a big volley-ball game in the school grounds. The girls, all the same small, stocky build, play in bare feet or in sandals in thick, flared skirts and white, embroidered blouses. They play with good humour, their identical pigtails bouncing on their backs.

As I write by candlelight Ricardo Quispe Mamani himself climbs up to my room. The visiting is unannounced, relaxed and natural. I think of the visiting in a Scottish west coast crofting community described by Alasdair MacLean in *Night Falls on Ardnamurchan*. There, you knew you had a night visitor when he was sitting beside you. Ricardo sits on my bed holding his radio to him. When we start to speak he turns it off.

He asks me my country and comments on my notebooks. I tell him I am a writer and that I was robbed in Cuzco Airport and lost camera, films and all my writing, so I have come to a tranquil place to try to remember.

'Mala gente. Bad people,' he says. 'Mala, mala gente.' He is slightly built, his shoulders hunched. Tonight his face is framed by one of the intricately patterned, knitted skull-caps with earflaps that are traditional wear here for the clear, cold nights. He has large, wide-set, brown liquid eyes and a broad, ready smile. He exudes gentleness and honesty and, for me, speaks slowly and deliberately.

'Here,' he says, 'we work. The men and the women and the children.' He shows me the callouses on his palms. 'We work hard because it is all done by hand. We have no machinery, no animals to help us, not even a donkey: we need all the land there is for ourselves. But it is better than robbing.'

'Yes, I think so.'

'Here on Amantani, there is no problem. You can leave everything, anywhere. No one will touch it.' He picks up a novel I'm reading. 'This book: if you lose it somewhere, someone will pick it up and return it to you. Once, in one house a tourist left passport, money, everything in the bed. The house owner found it and ran with it to the boat.' He smiles. 'The tourist was very happy.'

Roberto arrives and Ricardo tells him about my robbery. 'They do the same to us,' he continues. 'They do like this,' and he pulls his son's woollen hat over his eyes and frisks him. Roberto blinks and smiles, then picks up the novel and my small dictionary and balances them one in each hand. 'Feel the difference,' he tells his father.

The señora now arrives to be told the story. She skims through the novel which seems to fascinate them. (It wouldn't if they could read it: an overblown sci-fi called *Contact* by Carl Sagan. But beggars can't be . . .) She sits in silence for a few minutes, simply to breathe in the company of others, then goes and brings me my soup, followed by potatoes, onion and a fried egg. At half past seven it's curtains.

I drift off to sleep smelling the sweet smell of the straw mattress, but I'm woken by driving rain. There are no dogs here; the only sound is the weather.

All morning it pours. The lake has become a grey, forbidding sea. *Speak, Memory*. When the rain stops I set off for a walk in the cool, after-rain air.

Along the main trails, the width of a pavement with walls like bulwarks on each side, there's a constant traffic, involving all ages. Husband and wife pass, the wife either spinning or knitting; for the island economy depends on sales of its fine weaving and knitting. (The tiny straw baskets they weave are almost bird-like in their perfection.) Behind them tramp the children like miniature adults, small hoes sticking out of their bundles. From the high fields, figures come down the track laden with potatoes or with a bundle of mint, the scent of which lingers in the air after them. In the stillness you can hear calls from the hillside half a mile away. Some are calls to each other; some to the gringo. 'Hola!' they shout, 'Hola!'

I hear pronounced heavy breathing behind me. A small boy catches up with me. 'Dame caramelo. Give me a sweet.' I tell him I don't give to people who can't say please. He tuts disappointment. I repeat and he catches on with a flowery 'Por favor' and a heartfelt 'Gracias.'

Many of the children are shy: some girls pass, tilting their heads away from my greetings. But others, like the small boy I recently encountered, are hardened and bold. '¡Dame plata!' they shout. '¡Dame caramelo!', '¡Dame lapicero!' – Give me money/a sweet/a pen – their rough brown hands extended. It's just a try-on that's worked before, delivered like a statement, not with the desperation and dependency of the displaced, urban campesino child whose need has become so much greater. When it doesn't work they turn away, none the unhappier it would seem. At times I think of the first contacts the people of St Kilda had with the outside world. I imagine the same shyness, the same brazen demands.

The geography of the island is simple. On each side the inhabited coastal strip rises steeply from the water's edge; rises to the two volcanic peaks of Pachamama and Pachatata. 'Peaks' is actually to give the wrong impression, anywhere else they would be no more than hills; but on Amantani they give a commanding view of Lake Titicaca and make you feel as if you're on top of the world.

A trail marked with simple stone arches every half mile or so leads to Las Ruinas on top of each, but it's easy to lose yourself in the maze of secondary trails which weave between the small fields. The landscape reminds me of the west coast of Ireland, of Inishere, the smallest of the Aran Islands on which I once spent a few days – the same tradition of building walls to clear land as much as to protect. And everywhere you look there's evidence of the back-breaking work it's taken to create this landscape. Walls burst with volcanic stone, a rich, porous red, like vegetables that have flowered and spoiled.

Coming to the top of Pachamama, panting like a dog in the torrid heat and thin air, I trudge over a mass of grey shale, each shattered step clear in the silence. I look down the other side of the island on to tall fields of barley, stands of eucalyptus.

Pachamama has a round walled enclosure about sixty feet in diameter. The entrance has been filled with stones, but I can see a sunken area inside making a small arena, in the centre of which there's a red stone three feet high the shape of a cotton reel and, in a round black patch, evidence of a fire.

Pachamama, the mother, looks over to Pachatata, the father, its square enclosure obvious about three quarters of a mile away. More thick dry stone arches connect the two ruins and lead the eye into a singular landscape. Pachatata is a perfect high arc. From its stone quadrangle, fields ripple out in neat sections, organic as the ribs of a leaf. As elsewhere in Peru, this whole hillside has been ploughed by hand: the animal-drawn plough was unknown in Inca times and is still unsuitable for use in the Andes. Generally, though, the effect is one of stillness, of supreme design: it is only in passing a family raising picks over their heads to break the deep brown clods that you consider the huge effort which has made this landscape.

I pass through the small valley between the ruins, through a field where a group of women and children are shearing the small island sheep. It's like a pastoral. The older woman and two younger work while the three girls dance around, jump on and off walls, till my presence quells them.

A few fields have the remains of small sunken stone dwellings, intimate as those at Skara Brae. I sit on a flat stone in one – the straw thatched roof would just have cleared my head – imagining what was kept in the neat stone alcoves. It's cool in here, watching the green lizards' short bursts over the stones, feeling the sun's work on my ear tops.

'¿Inca ruinas?' I ask a man whose family are working in a row at the digging.

'Sí. Todo.'

Pachatata's square is larger than the circle, but has a similar arena; in the centre of it too the tell-tale black scar of a fire. From here you can see clearly the frieze of mountains around Lake Titicaca rising steeply from the water and the spits of land which thrust themselves towards Amantani. (In the far distance are the snow-capped peaks of the Bolivian Cordillera Real where I will be heading soon.) Taquile sits like a huge limpet on the peerless blue waters. The effect is such you would think a giant mountain range had been flooded and only the peaks are left showing above the waterline.

Walking down towards the pueblo again, seeing the roomy spread of small farms, the elegant eucalyptus trees which shade them, a handful of birds break from the tall lupins. They are shaped like giant kingfishers and in the sunlight they appear to be golden. Yes, not the bright, vivid yellow of yellow-hammers, but golden. Their call is like the peewit, but here it doesn't sound melancholy like those peewits over Scotland's moors and ruined crofts. Here its two-syllable song is for COLOUR: the yellow of the small flowers called solinas, which grow wherever is not cultivated, the bright green health of the plants, the light on the red volcanic rock and that glancing sapphire blue of the lake.

I am intrigued by the fires – the continuation of some ancient, Inca ceremony perhaps? – so when Ricardo climbs up to my room this evening, I am ready with questions.

He tells me the ruins have nothing to do with the Incas, that they were built after the Incas were here.

'But the Incas were here?' I ask.

'Yes, but they never left anything.'

'Then who built the ruins?'

'The people of Amantani after the Incas.'

'And what is their significance?'

Ricardo tells me they are part of a very ancient belief.

'That's still celebrated?' I advance slowly. 'I saw evidence of fires.'

'Yes. It is on the Day of Pachatata and Pachamama, the twentieth January each year. At midday all the people from Amantani dress up in traditional costume and they go up to the two centres. Everyone eats coca leaves and makes good prayers – oraciones – for one hour.'

'And when you pray, who are you praying to?'

'A Dios y a la tierra. To God and the earth.'

'And what do you pray for?'

'For the flowers, for growth, for our food.'

He explains there is a man called a curandero, a shaman, on both sites. After the prayers the curandero ritually burns coca leaves on the fire and everyone leaves the enclosures for a feast of specially prepared local food. The feast over, both groups descend into the valley where they dance and sing for about an hour. 'Without alcohol,' Ricardo assures me. 'We are not drunkards.' Then each dancer goes back to his own community.

'And what,' I ask, 'is the origin of this belief?'

'Many years ago the people worked the land.' This is a living tale told by a living flame. 'They worked hard but things wouldn't grow.

The plants bore little food. Then an old man came from Bolivia to Amantani. He burned coca and he prayed. And the plants grew and bore food. The ruins are for this man. I do not know how old this belief is, but it is very ancient. My father had it and his father and his father. I have it and Roberto has it.'

'And the Day of Pachatata and Pachamama – is it more important to you than Christmas?'

'Oh yes, much more. It is the most important day of the year for the people of Amantani.'

'I met a man at Machu Picchu who was a little bit Inca. He said the sun was his father, the earth was his mother, the water was his mother . . .'

'Yes, that is the Inca belief.'

'Do you believe in anything like that?'

'No, no. Nothing like that! Solamente en Dios y la tierra.'

I nod understanding and think of Hugh MacDiarmid's lines in 'Island Funeral' about the islanders being 'Priest-ridden by convention/And pagan by conviction.'

'The small stone houses I saw up there – are they Inca ruins?'

'No,' he says decisively. 'These were the houses of Los Hinteles.'

'Los Hinteles. Who were they?'

'They were the first people here, before the people of Amantani. They lived before the sun.'

'Before the sun,' I repeat matter-of-factly.

'Si, en la oscuridad antes del sol. In the dark before the sun. And when the sun appeared they all died and then the people who were to be the people of Amantani came from other islands, from peninsulas in the south . . .'

Ricardo shows great patience with me as I reach for the dictionary or, using a book and his long fingers, he makes the rituals clear to me. When his wife arrives to sit quietly on the end of the bed I tell her I've been working her husband very hard. Many questions. She smiles with pride.

And the golden bird? Its name in Quechua, the language of the family, the first language, is *ilako*.

I walk down the steep path to the harbour. The small fleet of Amantani boats with their distinctive green plumb-line idle there. I sit on a rock and listen to the water lap and the boys whistle as they pull their tin boats across the long sweep of the stony bay.

When I climb back up to the pueblo there's a meeting in progress. The square is full of islanders, the men in trilbies or baseball caps, the women with embroidered black shawls round their shoulders or over their heads.

I lean in the shade against the cool church wall and listen to the Quechua of the mayor, a small man in brown trilby, patterned jersey and jacket, deliver his weekly oration about island matters. He stands on a set of stone steps which run the length of the square. Beside him sit the other island dignitaries, the representatives of each of the six communities into which the island is divided. Around el alcalde (the mayor) there is a respectful, attentive silence. Behind him, behind the last of the houses, the ancient terraces, which his forebears have shaped and which now shape this community, rise up steeply to the rock escarpment dominating this side of the island. Left of it, the swell of Pachatata begins.

I continue my afternoon stroll.

From the tall shining broad-beans a little girl in pigtails, wearing a large floppy woollen hat like a flower, raises her head; a small hoe in her hand. A boy in a baseball cap runs to the wall: '¡Dame plata!' Just fishin'.

A small boy rounds up chickens with a stick twice as long as himself.

Two small, scruffy, dark brown pigs snort in their mud-pen.

Skirts make flashes of colour, passing through the green. Everyone carries something: potatoes, pails of water, oca – empty hands and backs are few.

Each family-sized field adds to the richness of its neighbours: the shiny, watery mass of barley heads next to the tall spears of broad-bean, the clumpy rows of oca with their bushy heads of clover-like leaves, the delicate purples of pea-flowers. And all those different greens: the green of rawness, of ripeness, the yellowing green of what's flowered and past, the silvery green of the eucalyptus with the last light on it.

This is a landscape that is always drawing you into itself. On the Day of Pachatata and Pachamama, you too might pray for its continuance. But I wonder, how is such an intricate landscape realised?

Tonight Ricardo draws the island in my notebook – two small circles for Pachamama and Pachatata – and divides it like a pie-chart into four main sections or suyos. Three of these are allocated to different crops and the fourth lies fallow. The crops – puro papa (potatoes), pura oca (sweet potatoes) and trigo cebada (wheat) – rotate each year. Each family has their own fields in each suyo, but everyone works together on the same crop.

'And who decides which suyo will grow what?'

'Los Envarados. Ten men chosen from one of the six communities. It is an obligation to accept if you are chosen. No, there is no election; the choices are usually obvious. These ten men change each year. Their duty is to take care of the island. Cuidar la isla.' Spoken with pride and affection.

'It sounds like a good democracy.'

Ricardo smiles broadly. 'Yes, it is.'

Halfway through a morning's work, I climb down for a coffee. The children's room is below mine and I can see clothes strung from the ceiling, shoes flung beneath the bed, blankets cast aside. At the end of Roberto's small bed are cardboard boxes for shelves and his tiny array of treasures: a miniature straw boat, a small pottery bull, a coloured-in picture of an eagle.

I cross the small vegetable patch to the open toilet with its wedged branch support. The pen of guinea pigs squeaks twice.

Juanita sits in the kitchen and looks up with her embarrassed half-smile/half-laugh when I bend down and step inside.

The stone-built kitchen hut which stands alone is the hub of the house. It is about nine feet square, its walls and thatched ceiling black with soot. At one end is the raised stone floor which at one time must have been a sleeping area. Now it's where the family sit each evening cosy on a rug in the dim smoky light; like the black house dwellers in the Western Isles preferring the warmth of the hearth to the luxury of space.

Along one wall is a low stone table-top, no different from those in the houses of Los Hinteles. On it there's a paraffin stove for immediate needs (my coffees!), but most food is boiled or fried on a metal construction the size of a large upturned basin which has two openings into which long pieces of wood are fed. On wooden shelves lie the round, blackened pots and the ends of vegetables, herbs, a bowl of eggs and one of rice. On the stone floor is a charred-looking frying pan. The musty smell of concentrated earth, which the people also faintly carry, stirs a memory of dipping my head deep into the darkness of empty potato bunkers on farm holidays as a child.

Juanita is fourteen. She tells me she doesn't have to go to school after twelve. She gives her half-laugh and tells me she doesn't know how old people generally are when they get married. Last night I remember a young man running past me with a very animated 'Buenas tardes'. I saw him later, standing at a meeting of walls, a shy girl keeping her distance. Island courting.

It's Roberto's thirteenth birthday. He is small for his age with large brown eyes, a toothy smile, sloping shoulders and a readiness to please. His uncertainty with strangers is nothing like Juanita's, more the island child's natural reserve.

During his lunch-hour I give him the last orange, a biro and three lollipops, all I can muster, and wish him a happy birthday. 'Muchas gracias,' he says. 'Muchas gracias.' Like a miniature adult, his head bows slightly and his small hand comes up for a firm adult shake.

In the square I hear the schoolchildren enthusiastically chant one to fifty as I start a late afternoon walk away from the Pachas into the suyo of trigo cebada.

The main path splits the cultivated area. Above me the reddish escarpment and the red stone of the terraces contrasts with all the fresh greens sketched in long lines. Below, I look down on the differing surfaces, the differing states of ripeness from light green through to gold. The late sun setting over the mainland lays a bright path over the water, coming right in at the small bay. A fisherman is silhouetted there, standing on a rocky promontory. The light gives a honeyed sheen to the barley and wheat. I sit on a smooth stone and watch yellow-breasted finches in their dipping flights across the still-warm air.

Following an ancient rhythm people are wending their way home before the light fails. I hear the panting of a barefoot woman behind me. She looks about fifty, but bent over and weather-beaten it's hard to tell. She rests her sack on the wall, reties it and is off, the bulging sack covering her head and her thighs.

'Enjoying the view?' It's a young man in sweat top and tracksuit bottoms.

'Oh, yes, it's beautiful with the sun on the wheat.'

He laughs concurrence. 'Do you have islands as beautiful as this in your country?'

'Yes, I think so. But not at this moment! At this moment there is nowhere more beautiful than this in the whole world.'

He laughs again, and as the light is fading we walk back to the village, past small boys running hurdy-gurdies; he teaching me plant names for which I can find no translation.

My last day, I walk right around the island.

On its far side the ringing pitch of two men chiselling draws me over. They wear trilbies over woollen hats and the stones they quarry are large as suitcases.

'Hello. It's hot. Too hot for walking, never mind working.'

'Yes, it is. Are you walking round the island?'

'Yes, it's beautiful.'

'Yes, it is. We're working.' And back they go, their clear notes alone punctuating the silence.

At the archway which divides the suyo of puro papa, where women sit on their hunkers, feet planted in the soft earth, and hack small potatoes out with their hoes, and the suyo of pura oca with its neat rows of bunched, dark green leaves, carriers stop and rest their bundles on the wall. I stop too; climb the natural embankment and look over the homeward stretch down to the pueblo.

There is a stillness over the waters, a stillness which stretches to the most distant mountain-top. Reach out: what is not included in this lucid air? And look for long and, like one of Cézanne's views of the Mediterranean, the water seems as much a vertical blue screen as a horizontal lake.

A man with what appears to be two sacks of potatoes on his back stops and looks up to where I sit.

'Hola. Buenos dias. ¿Que tal?'

'Muy bien, gracias.'

'¿Qué pais, amigo?' This is one place where amigo doesn't sound like derision.

'Escocia.'

'Escocia,' he nods. 'Bueno. ¿Cuantos dias aqui en Amantani?'

'Mañana, una semana. Me gusta mucho Amantani.'

'Si. Es tranquilo. Hay aire libre, ameno.'

He trips off on his way. I look up and sense Amantani floating in this stillness, in a blue limpidity.

Ricardo comes up to my room unannounced as usual. We shake hands and he sits.

'You go tomorrow?' he says.

'Yes. I don't want to but I must.' Again I tell him my route. He repeats it to himself as if he has trouble lodging it in his mind. 'Puno. La Paz. Lima.' Slowly, deliberately, as if these places are remote, unlikely destinations. Even saying them, never mind introducing Brazil, I feel an extravagance, a showy greed for experience.

'Tomorrow,' he says, 'we will sail round the island. The whole way round.' His finger makes a wide circle.

'Muy bueno,' I say. 'It'll be like a holiday.'

He smiles. 'You go tomorrow. Can you not stay another day to sail round the island?'

Ah, Ricardo, I can see it. You at the helm of the small, wooden sailing boat with the green line around it. It will be called *Flor de* something. There is just the sound of the water lapping gently at the prow, the occasional laughter from Claris and Victoria. At each suyo I say, 'Trigo cebada, puro papa . . . Muy bonita,' and you smile and nod, proud of your island and my delight in it.

'Will you come back?' he asks.

'Ah, it's very expensive between Scotland and here.'

He shakes his head. Yes, he understands that.

I show him how much I've written here, how good a place it has been for me. He smiles. 'All on Amantani?'

'All this,' I say, flicking through the pages.

Señora Mamani arrives, edging into the room with her duster, waging her constant war against the flies. She sits on the edge of the second bed. She has a flat, round face with eyes close together and a wide smile. It is a face I have seen on Inca pottery. She is the quiet and strong mother figure, her full breasts kept half in check by a curtain pin on her blouse. But tonight both she and Ricardo are pale, earth-tired – the cost of the landscape.

'Muy cansada,' she says. 'Mucho trabajo con puras papas.'

Ricardo bends his head and puts a hand to a yawn that seems to come from deep inside himself. Always there have been unembarrassed silences between us, but this time they are filled with their exhaustion.

Ricardo takes a finished biro to bits with tired fascination. He looks up at me. 'Ah, Tomas, tomorrow, amigo, when you are not here and I am alone, I will be sad.' He says this twice.

And twice I say it and mean it: 'Me too, Ricardo. Me too.'

And sometimes things don't work out the way you expect them to. When I walk out of the house and through the square on my way to a final peaceful meditation at my favourite bay view in trigo cebada, the young man from last night comes out of a doorway with a large cassette in his arms.

'Going for a walk?'

'Yes.'

'Same place? Come on.'

He tells me there's no work for him in Amantani, certainly not for the whole year, and he must go to Puno. He works in the craft business there, making rugs from alpaca. As he talks a train of small boys returning from school tramps behind us to the beat of the folk-pop tape. They wear the grey regulation jerseys common throughout Peru and carry small shoulder-satchels.

When we arrive at the spot the cassette is placed on a flat stone and the boys, all high from après-school, gather round, their bright, smiling faces meaning mischief to us both. They laugh Quechua at me while one removes the volume control and drops it some distance away. They run off laughing like parrots as my companion shouts after them in disgust. I sense his slighted dignity and mouth some platitude about boys being boys the world over.

I ask him his name again. Last night I had no idea how to pronounce it and assumed it was pure Quechua. He writes it for me. 'DISLLOKEY': the double 'l' in Spanish gives a 'yi' sound. Still I am puzzled. 'You know,' he explains, 'they have them on the radio. People call me it because I'm always talking. My real name is Martin Callata Calsin.'

'Ah.' We nod at each other.

'Is your country democratic or communist?' he asks.

Explaining the politics of my country, the standing of my country, the relationship of my country to England, to Britain, to Mrs Thatcher is one of the great quagmires facing the Scottish traveller. Not something I want to talk about at this moment. 'Democratic,' I answer conclusively.

Then the sun is gone and it's suddenly cold and the distant mountains are their night time black cut-out. Well, I think, that was it. Last night was really the night I must value – the night when I was aware of all the gifts Amantani has borne me. We start off back to the pueblo.

I turn around; one last look.

In one dip in the mountains, where the sun has just sunk, there is a red volcanic brilliance. Above it, is a cloud so dense it appears to be like a girder, half of it molten. An orange swathe covers the centre of the island; wings of red cloud hang in the still-blue sky. I turn back to the path; before me, a bright full moon seals Amantani's late gift.

Back at the house Ricardo immediately pays me another visit. It is as though he wants to get my record straight before I leave.

This is not paradise either. We discuss the lack of work, of land. Land passes from father to son: his is split between himself and his father. His father grows enough to 'export', while all Ricardo's produce is for the family. His four sisters have all had to leave to find work in Lima, all in artesania. And if in Amantani there is a season without rain, he also must work in the leather trade in Lima for three or four months to support his family. No, he doesn't like Lima: 'Muchos robos en Lima.' I see the metallic lid of its sky next to Amantani's perfect blue.

'If it rains in Amantani there is food,' he says, summing up. 'If not, triste la vida aquí.'

So I see Amantani at its most fruitful; all the crops shining and tall. But there is a margin of sufficiency which demands vigorous work and quarter-mastering; earth that takes its tribute of sweat.

Roberto has failed to deliver the promised trout. The señora sighs relief when I tell her more soup will suffice.

I walk down the broadest thoroughfare on the island, that which leads to the harbour. In the early sun the quinoa glows a light yellowish-green like cabbage on the turn.

The boatman wears a traditional thick navy woollen three-piece suit over a white woollen shirt. 'I don't want to leave this island,' I tell him.

The boat fills up with sacks of produce; with islanders wearing faded trilbies over their woollen skull-caps; with mothers and babies. Their voices are never raised in greeting – the whole week I can't remember a shout bar the occasional 'hola'. These are island people with an island self-sufficiency in their deep brown eyes. Silence does not panic them. When one kneels on the seat I see heels cracked like earth and, on some, toes that seem almost to be growing together like tubers. The hard life of the earth is the life they know and the one they want to live. When Disllokey nods to me this morning it is with a distant seriousness, as if he is already bracing himself to lose his identity in the harshly impersonal world across the water.

A Small Matter of Perspective
LA PAZ

'Well, I burnt all my writing. It's no *big deal*.'

'Huh?' Had I misheard? With his amused, unshocked expression, his bush-hat set so jauntily on the back of his head, this American was difficult to take.

'I'm just trying to get some perspective here,' he said as I twisted the last coldness from my beer bottle. Our solitary eyes had arranged this meeting at the restaurant of Hostal Rosario, La Paz. Now I was thinking my loneliness would be far less bruising.

'Perspective?' I gulped.

'Exactly. Look at Hemingway . . .'

'Oh, aye.'

'Yeah. His first wife, Hadley, left a whole valise crammed with manuscripts in a railway carriage. And Malcolm Lowry . . .'

'First draft of *Under the Volcano* lost when his shack in British Columbia went on fire. And Carlyle's *History of the French Revolution* that the maid lit the fire with . . .' I knew all these; had already played with them in my mind, from the most inconsequential (Mickey Spillane's 'another three days' work never hurt anyone') to the most tragic: the story of Joseph de Jussieu and his search for the fever tree. I reached for my notebook. 'Here, though, listen to this one. In 1735, Joseph de Jussieu, aged thirty-one, set out to find the fever tree which cured malaria. In 1761, that's twenty-six years later' – the American nodded tiredly – 'he was preparing to sail home from Buenos Aires. The night before his ship sailed, Jussieu left all his material in the care of a servant with strict instructions to guard it because it was of great value. The next morning the servant and the baggage were gone. Jussieu wandered through South America for the next ten years. In 1771 he returned to Paris, a broken man. He was committed to an asylum where he died soon afterwards.'

119

I looked up, my eyes wide, expecting to find in his an echo of the chill of waste. But there was only a slight, impatient nodding. His story was obviously more important than Joseph de Jussieu's – or mine. Perspective.

His story. Well, it turned out he used to be a 'pretty successful writer', but then he found he was just getting into 'things that were too weird.' So he just stopped – 'made that decision' – burned everything he had written and now he just took pictures. 'Just taking pictures' was supported by a philosophical edifice that took two bottles of beer to explain and provided lots of opportunity for amused, patronising glances. It was like spending an evening with a character from *Catcher in the Rye*, one Holden Caulfield would have designated 'a phoney from some crummy place like Des Moines or somewhere.' Once, though, his cool slipped.

'I was climbing up through this favela; I shouldn't even have been there. Anyway, I came to this old cemetery and against one wall was this kind of beehive grave affair and someone had broken into one of the graves and pulled out this baby's coffin and smashed it open. Well, I've never even seen a dead body before – imagine, what with the bones, the shroud and the flies; if I hadn't had the camera between me and it, I don't think I could have looked. God, I don't know if I should even be talking about it.' In the end we both felt more comfortable talking about stealing. But whaddayaknow?

'Same thing happened to me in Arequipa. In a café. Someone picks up a bill from the floor, opens it. "Is it yours?" they ask. Then I look. My camera, months of film – gone. And this happens to me after spending five months in Brazil – in Rio, Salvador, f'chrissake. Crazy.'

'So?'

'So, I run out the café. A woman points one way but I see a man with a bulge in his coat and I leap on him. O-o-o-h, man, do I feel the adrenalin! He just gave right up without a struggle. They do if you can catch them. No, Peru's just not the place to be at the moment.'

And why was he in La Paz?

He had been in advertising. This was how it happened. 'I was doing a lay-out of a woman in a mink coat and I'm trying to get the flesh tones right and I'm asking myself: hey, how is it every time I do this it comes out wrong? Then it dawns on me: the model is a *Barbie doll*, f'chrissake! Yea, a real Barbie doll. I gave up the job there and then and headed for Brazil. I'm not ambitious now. I just want to

keep travelling. I go home and people are either getting divorced or
remarried and they haven't seen through it all yet. But I just arrive
in La Paz and I think, whew, here I am.'

'For what?'

'Well, I was five months in Brazil and I thought then, if I want to
get further into South America I need Spanish. I came here briefly
last year and found it the most comfortable of cities to walk about in,
so I'm here for two months to learn Spanish.'

'And then?'

'Who knows?' The line, thrown away with a toss of the hand,
was a familiar blend of contrived ease and arrogance. The status of
Top Traveller is one that is self-appointed and only has currency
among the knots of those tacking their way through the continent
with varying degrees of frustration and ill luck. My American
'friend' basked in this small lonely pool and appeared to revel in
the uncertainties of the traveller's life.

Not this traveller. Oh no, not this traveller.

Not that there had been anything problematical about the journey
to La Paz – just the normal anxieties. My gut, after a period of
glorious dependability on a diet of potatoes, was bailing everything
out again, spurred on by a meal of *Lomo* (pork) *a lo Gordon Blyed*
from Puno International Restaurant. A diet of imodium with
imodium chasers had meant my moneybelt sat more comfortably
around my shrinking waist. In fact, with my spartan diet and
my gentleman's bag which could accommodate only the tiniest of
souvenirs (a freedom I thought, compared to others' great domed
rucksacks), I began to feel like some travelling ascetic, roaming
through 'the vast cinema of sensation.'

It was an often spectacular bus ride on which the waters of Lake
Titicaca were rarely out of sight. The lake has no drainage system
– excess water flows south to the marshes of Lake Poopo then
evaporates into sand – so the last of Peru was a sodden plain
fringed by snow-capped mountains. Here colourless villages and
mud houses, seemingly built at random, scraped a tired sustenance
from the soil and the scrappy flocks of sheep and isolated, tethered
cattle. With Amantani fresh in my mind it seemed to me that more
than the cattle were tethered here.

It was some relief to come to the Bolivian town of Copacabana with
its huge white cathedral. From there, after a change of buses and yet

another lunch-time fast, the road climbed up into a bare landscape of mountains sweeping into each other, before it settled into the endless vistas of the high altiplano, a treeless puna 3,962 metres above sea level; home for llamas, alpacas and the Aymara Indians. It was a strange, discomfiting and disorientating landscape. I thought about the early Scottish settlers of the Great Plains of America who endured terrible confusions because of the pure space they had never experienced before, except perhaps at sea. Many hallucinated that they were shrinking or else expanding to fill it. Here houses looked to me like Monopoly chips: seeing a man cycling over the pathless tundra I scanned hopelessly for a possible point of reference he might have. Then the shanty-towns began to thicken till suspiciously flimsy concrete blocks announced La Paz which sat cradled deep in the mountains, a crush of modest skyscrapers and stone churches, glowing red in the late sunshine.

After the stasis of Amantani, the joys of travel: movement, new sights, a new country, a new capital, fellow-travellers with whom to swop notes about other countries, other capitals. And La Paz was a very attractive capital, the highest in the world, built on hills, walkable. I thought of cold nights in Edinburgh and went everywhere with a relaxation I had rarely felt in Peru.

'Our position as an extension of the working class is to ally ourselves with the miners and to fight the government's relocation programme,' read a banner outside the university, which was on strike. Its forecourt was taken up by miners and students writing such signs, while women and children were stopping traffic, thrusting paper signs over windscreens: 'We need to eat.'

Mining and the condition of miners has been a running sore in Bolivia since the colonial period when Indians were herded off for certain death in the silver mines of Potosí, at that time the wealthiest city in South America. I had planned to take a train there; to head south and see more of South America. Yet I milled around the edge of the crowd at the demonstration feeling completely detached. It began to pour and I took shelter in a basement café. I wrote a few postcards – I had more faith in Bolivia's postal service than Peru's – and wondered what I was doing here.

I had worked hard while I was on Amantani, reconstructing the bones of my experiences without the satisfaction of cradling them in apposite language. Yet I felt at last I had straightened out the time that had buckled when I lost all my writing. Now I was in a position to move on; but something had taken root deeper than the superficialities of travelling – a feeling that my story was not here, that something was drawing me back to Peru. After the initial decision to continue my trip had come the fight to quell bitterness. The third stage back to health would need to be an attempt to make sense of what had happened to me and why.

The effort of understanding was not being made by me alone. For months now, *El Comercio*, Peru's leading daily, had been running articles on Peruvian identity which it called 'the theme of our time.' It was the 450th anniversary of the birth of the Inca Garcilaso de la Vega and a double-page spread in *El Comercio* proclaimed, 'Garcilaso, simbolo de la peruanidad.' Garcilaso, the son of an Inca princess and a conquistador, was the author of *Comentarios Reales* which for four centuries provided the fullest and richest account of Inca society. He had argued that Spain and Inca Peru had reached a parallel stage of social and cultural development at the point of the conquest, allowing the possibility of fusion. The subsequent dismemberment of Inca society showed the faint enthusiasm the Spaniards had for this opportunity, yet it was such an idea which had given the term 'mestizo' a dignity beyond its racist translations of 'half-breed' or 'half-caste'.

In the article Garcilaso was touted as the first American and his work seen as the starting point of 'a sensibility absolutely new, absolutely Peruvian.' If so, it was a sensibility developed largely in exile: Garcilaso left Peru when he was fourteen and his history was written decades later. I had read similar claims for 'the Peruvian sensibility' of the poet Cesar Vallejo on the back of an edition of his first collection, *Los Heraldos Negros*. This was said to be 'the first Peruvian book of poetry that does not make tribute to a colonial aesthetic.' It was published in 1918, over four hundred years after the conquest, and five years later Vallejo began his miserable exile in Paris.

However, titles taken at random from a bookshop in Lima had made it obvious to me that being a Peruvian was a more problematical condition than the simplicity of the Garcilaso/mestizo solution would allow: *Peru in Crisis*, *Who Are We?*, *Violence and Crisis of Values in Peru*, *The Labyrinth of Crisis*, *The Peruvian Nation – The Trajectory of a Fallacy*, *Peru in the 90s – A Possible Road*, *Reports from Anonymous Peru*. (Peru: the very name arose from a misunderstanding on the part of the Spaniards when Indians told them the name of a river: originally, it was known simply as 'New Castille'.) Such a fragile sense of identity, such a ceaseless, hopeless questing, I could not help but sympathise with: how many books had I seen which asked Who Are The Scots?

I sat in the café as the rain showed no sign of letting up and drew up a short list of people I had met with whom I could air my perplexity. My journey, I realised now, was not one that had begun at fixed point 'A' and would run to 'B': crossing space – by canoe or donkey or *in the footsteps of* – was not what it was about. I felt the whole continent slipping through my fingers, leaving me Peru – a claustrophobic room filling up with terrorism, hyper-inflation, drugs and thieves. If, as Shiva Naipaul commented, 'All travel is a form of extinction,' then Peru seemed a perfect place to experience it.

Rain bounced off the steps at the café's doorway. It triggered an image of a diver shooting to the surface with a pinhead of breath, his arm like Excalibur. In his hand he holds the precious end of an old frayed piece of rope, the kind pedlars sold piles of on Lima's Abancay – the beginnings of an answer. A grand image I have to admit, but then re-entering that room still gave me some anxiety: as my American 'friend' surely recognised, I was in need of 'positive visualisation.'

When it stopped raining, I walked streets like rivers to a travel agent and bought a ticket for a flight back to Lima – a real twitcher, in search of 'B'.

PART THREE

¿Que te parece Peru?

'A Wacky Bunch of Ass-Holes'
and other Problems
LIMA

I

I had two opportunities to study the Peruvian coastline south of Lima. The first was when I took the bus to Nazca and then on to Arequipa. The second when I returned to Lima after La Paz. For neither would I have given my right arm.

The coastal region of Peru is one of the driest regions in the world. Lima itself averages only about four centimetres of rain a year; yet a heavy slate sky hangs over it, often for days. This plays tricks with the recent arrival who thinks a good shower is all that's needed to clear the air and in my case keeps on imagining spots of rain falling on his head.

Cultivation of fields of cotton, sugar-cane, maize, alfalfa and the vine is only made possible by rivers flowing from the Andes to the Pacific. Oases would I suppose be the correct name for these valleys, but there is a picturesqueness I associate with the term which did not fit the Peruvian coastline. For, apart from a few shady chakras (small farms), the prevailing imagery which settled in my mind was a depression of shanty-towns – box-like straw houses where women sat in dark doorways and dogs sidled past children with baseball hats and ragged nylon shorts – set amid great expanses of barren land that did not have the clean lines or the mystique of the desert, but were covered in unromantic rubble.

The bus had passed by stretches of beach so straight and for such a distance that I felt this was the lonely knife-edge of the world. From high, twisting roads, I looked down into valleys where men and women were bent over grey fields, tending, coaxing some green from the dust. Yet great civilisations had thrived here long before the Inca empire earned its title of Tahuantinsuyu by uniting the

126

coastal and highland people of Peru in an empire that was to last only a century.

Mochica, Nazca, Chimu: I'll admit they sounded like chocolate bars to me. In Nazca, though, I had seen *the Lines*. For almost forty years Maria Reich had studied these huge stylised figures – the spider, the whale, the humming-bird, the monkey, the 'astronaut' – which cover five hundred square kilometres of a desert that is drier than the Sahara. She 'discovered' the figures and mapped them out, mostly by standing on a pair of step-ladders in the searing heat. A journalist told me her father had brought her and her doctor sister up with the feeling they had to do something worthwhile with their lives. The scale of her energy and obsessional commitment have made her a paragon of European involvement and fascination with the mystery, the *otherness* of South America.

From Nazca I drove out into the desert with a slow-talking young American who was way past his sell-by date as far as travel was concerned. Every so often he drawled, 'There's a line,' and, 'Oh lookee. There's another line.'

In the afternoon I took another tour, this time with Erich, an Austrian who farmed in Manitoba because in Manitoba his nearest neighbour was three kilometres away. He had come through Ayacucho, Sendero territory, and his bus had been stopped. 'They just talked and wanted a contribution. Their weapons were really old. One small boy with them pointed to someone's shoes and they had to give them over.' Erich smiled at the memory. In jeans, boots and a T-shirt with a bright-eyed smile for everyone and not a passport or chequebook in sight, he was the most natural traveller I met.

The tour consisted of me, Erich and a fat taxi-driving guide under a stetson, and was to Chauchilla, an open cemetery out in the red desert. For fifteen hundred years the skeletons had lain there, some huddled like the sad family groups I had seen on the streets of Lima. The dry desert air had preserved scraps of material, rope and hair. The fat guide picked up a weave of hair the length of a man and, holding it over his head, let the desert wind carry it. Then he laid it like a unravelled wreath across four white skulls. That short ritual was the strongest image I took from the dispiriting coastal journey I had first made soon after my arrival in Peru.

This time, though, I was only going part of the way to Nazca, and not by bus but in the comfort of a Toyota Range Rover with Toni

Anderson. Toni had a senior position in Action Aid, an independent charity which had two main projects in Peru: one near Huaraz and one below Ayacucho. These were irrigation projects designed to increase crop yields so that farmers could afford to have their children attend school, and afford school books, rather than work the land and tend the cattle.

Tall, clear-eyed and capable, Toni was one of those who had found a tangible happiness in her mid-thirties living and working in Peru. She found Peruvians kind and generous, full of laughter in spite of their hardships. She loved to get out of Lima and into the varying countrysides of Peru with their differing climates, and she shared her delight for Peruvian food, music and burning sunshine with the long-limbed enthusiasm of an adolescent. 'Yes,' she said when I had told her how badly I had failed as a coolly objective observer, 'Peru has a habit of drawing you in.' By the guts.

While in Lima I stayed in the leafy suburb of San Isidro with the husband from whom Toni was separated. Alan had stayed in Lima to be near their two children, Emma and Jamie, teaching English in a girls' school surrounded by high fences. In his spare time he painted strong portraits and pictures with a personal iconography culled from his time in Peru.

Some commentator once asked the pertinent question that if one person had read nothing but Susan Sontag on the Soviet Union in the last thirty years and another nothing but the *Reader's Digest*, which one would be closer to the truth? Toni and Alan offered the same conundrum regarding Peru. Whereas Toni was all bright brown-eyed enthusiasm and encouragement – 'Do it! Do it! Do it!' – Alan enjoyed giving me dire warnings about everything.

'Don't put your money there,' he pounced, pointing to my neck pouch. 'They'll slit that easily. And isn't that wallet a little obvious?' When I left Lima the first time, he tapped my shoulder-bag: 'Mmm, they're going to love that.'

Alan sported the rather cynical view that people, gringos, liked living in Peru because they could use external problems to excuse their own inadequacies: 'You can always blame it on Peru.' However, scratching the top of his peeling head and underscoring his thrusting views with a mordant sense of humour, I found him comfortingly Scottish, and he did furnish me with the occasional telling detail. For instance during the postal strike which was in operation when I arrived in Lima, you could still buy stamps, post your letters, as many as you wanted – and have them burnt with the rest of the mail sacks!

Chincha, halfway to Nazca, was a typical town of this coastal region: flat-roofed, whitewashed houses, fruit and vegetable stalls narrowing the heavily rutted streets still further, and an elegant stand of royal palms in its central square. Toni needed to see the police in Chincha about a road accident she had been involved in a couple of days before. Her business at the police station eventually concluded, we dined in a large, airy restaurant on the fruits of the sea – a large plate of piquant ceviche: uncooked fish marinated in lemon juice and hot pepper, served with corn-on-the-cob, sweet potatoes and onions; a recipe that has been served here for a thousand years. I thought of Ricardo's insistence on the richness of the Peruvian coast.

Two young policemen from the morning joined us. Both wore T-shirts now and were boyish in their affability. They told us Chincha was a good posting: that strings were pulled for it. But even here they were aware of Sendero; had even heard that local schoolteachers were members of it. Down the coast the small town of Pisco had swollen from four thousand inhabitants to twelve thousand, as fear drove people down from the Sendero stronghold of Ayacucho. But the fear was closing in. A few weeks before in Cañete, a few miles back up the coast, eight policemen had been killed when terrorists broke into the police station. However the incident which had depressed them most had happened at about the same time in Uchiza in the midst of the narco-trafficking area in north-central Peru. The police station had been attacked by Sendero. Three emergency phone calls had been put through to a government minister in Lima who had assured the station help was on its way. They were wiped out. Certainly these stories were a far cry from Erich's tale of the rather down at heel 'Dad's Army' organisation wanting nothing more than to put their case for revolution.

'Ah, you must taste a good pisco before you go.' Pisco, a white grape brandy similar to tequila, is the Peruvian equivalent to Scotland's own uisge bheatha, the water of life. Like all such spirits the world over, it is better to have it chosen for you by an aficionado who will begin your education by rubbishing all your previous experience. 'Ah, no, pah! That is not the real pisco, the good pisco. Now this . . .' And your enjoyment will be eased by your determination not to disappoint the smiling, slightly nodding face which shares the moment with you.

After this ritual, warming in both senses of the word, one of the young policemen insisted on driving the Toyota back to the station. Once he had parked it, he sat for a moment, like a child fingering the play of the wheel, then turned and asked me: '¿Qué te parece Chincha?'

Dreams. Nightmares. Realities.

II

One of the acutest observers I met in Peru on these nightmares, dreams and realities was a friend of Toni's, a forty-nine-year-old former radical priest from Los Angeles, Mark Richard Day. Mark had spent six years working with farm workers in California and immigrants in LA, but he was now an independent journalist currently working for ABC in Lima. I had met him during my first stint in Lima, at which time he gave me the valuable but now largely redundant advice: 'Well, if you're not already a registered paranoid about your luggage, you'd better become one.'

His maid let me into his secure, white washed apartment from a small courtyard splashed with geraniums. He was laid up recovering from hepatitis, caught, he imagined, from ice-cream bought on the street. 'I know it too, never eat anything you can buy on the street.' Mark's comments could be as doomy as Alan's, but there was not far behind them an awareness of the surreal in Peruvian life, the possibility of humour. The hepatitis had claimed ten pounds from him, and he wanted to lose more, but he had a broad open face which carried his weight, and puckered like a puppy's in seriousness or lit up like a man's half his age when he smiled.

Mark had heard about my robberies in Cuzco and wanted to speak to me for an article he was writing about tourism. For my part, I wanted to talk to him about the collusion that exists in Peru regarding such robberies; the acceptance of a culture of thievery. It was, we agreed, a way to survive in an underdeveloped, debt-ridden society and the deeper the crisis, the more thievery became entrenched.

'It's a pervasive morality problem,' said Mark, adjusting his dressing-gown and leaning forward on the couch. I recognised in him some of Barry's restless energy. 'I see it as a coastal phenomenon, a mercantile thing. They have this admiration for *viveza*. It means being clever, shrewd, smart in business dealings. It's a mark of distinction to be able to outsmart a person. And of course the Indians who come down from the mountains aren't that way, but they become so.'

Mark had lived for three and a half years in Lima and said that if anything drove him out it would be this constant wearing away, taking advantage.

'Of course Peruvians do have some historical justification for their melancholy. The conquest here was more bitter than anywhere else in South America. And their experience of authority structures, from the Incas to the colonial systems, means that if you want anything done here you have to go to the top and scream. It's also made them passive-aggressive: they go in for things like thieving in a sneaky way. Generally, if you challenge them they fade away.' Apart from the desperate that is: like the robber who clubbed a gringo on a bus outside Nazca on the night of March 14, then shot through the head a young Peruvian woman who had dared to protest.

Mark saw the events surrounding Uchiza on March 27, when Sendero took over the police post after a four-hour battle and executed the three commanding officers in the main square, as symptomatic of the Peruvian identity problem. 'It just showed that a lot of Limeños couldn't care about ten cholos. As long as the war doesn't come to their front door they don't give a shit. It was also an indication of a failure of will: the corruption of the police, the lack of the presence of government; a government that's now on the defensive, but not in any dignified way.'

Like most people I spoke with, Mark saw the APRA government in large part to blame for the despondency. APRA, the American Popular Revolutionary Alliance Party, had once been seen as the party favouring agricultural reform and economic progress. It had been proscribed for a time and its ascendancy to power in 1985 under the youthful Alan Garcia, 'President of all Peruvians', had been marked by a huge graffiti/mural campaign: 'ALAN CAMBIARA EL PERU.' Alan will change Peru. In Chivay, and countless other small towns, most large buildings had the APRA sign in red letters six feet high. Because of its populist rhetoric and its historical reputation, people had thought APRA might be able to solve some of the urgent economic problems Peru faced. But now these signs mocked the people who painted them, for the government was corrupt and recognised as such, sending money out of the country, guilty of nepotism and ineptitude. It had effectively left a power vacuum and the high moral ground to Sendero.

'Sure, Peru's a victim of structural, Third World problems and of the fall in prices of mining and oil, but this government has no control over anything. It was supposed to be all good things – anti-imperialist, pro-agriculture – but the president has bought three new homes since he's been in power. People want to know where he got the money from. It's the same thing, from shoeshine boy to president, everyone's got the attitude of doing a shitty job. *Lamentablamente*. Have you noticed that's one of the favourite words here? *Lamentablamente*.'

'Haven't actually; but I can see that it could easily have become one of mine.' Mark flashed me a brief smile then concluded sadly, 'Peruvians have no pride, no faith in Peruvians. The people are oppressing themselves and each other.' And while the APRA government vacillated and weakened, there were other parties pondering the shorter solution to one of Peru's great problems.

In the Upper Huallaga valley, cocaine valley, the American government was considering spraying SPIKE, 'the magic bullet'; a defoliant which would attack the roots of all woody plants in the area. Comparisons with the use of Agent Orange in Vietnam had meant that even the American manufacturers were against such use of their product and had refused to sell any more of it to the government, who were now thinking of buying the patent. Mark compared the situation to the words of General Westmoreland: '"We've got to kill this village to save it." And you know,' Mark continued, 'the classic thing to say is that the Peruvian government will never allow it. Christ, these bastards are so corrupt they'll let you pave the valley with concrete if you pay them enough!' Mark enjoyed laughter and laughed when I did, his blue eyes bright behind his glasses.

The Americans would no doubt argue that all other measures to tackle the drug problem at source had failed. The 1983 aid money, intended to persuade peasants to grow alternative crops, was a total, predictable failure: what other crop has a cash yield approaching that of cocaine? And the American seven million dollars for drug enforcement looked a pitiful sum set against an eight hundred million dollar drug industry. 'Eight hundred million dollars buys a lot of policemen on forty five dollars a month,' as Mark succinctly put it.

Sendero were also now closely involved in the narcotrafficking, protecting peasants' crops from the US agents. 'In the Third World,' Mark observed, 'the drug industry is enigma surrounded by dilemmas. The Incas offered coca leaves to the gods and today nine million Peruvians chew the leaf. Banning its use here would be seen as similar to banning bread. The situation must be tackled in the US.'

Sendero, however, was a problem Peru faced alone. To the outsider – Mark at his most existentially comic – they were 'a wacky bunch of ass-holes'. He was in a better situation to know than most, having allowed himself to be captured by them for a week for an article he was writing. 'Not an experience I'd like to repeat. They're fundamentalists, like Pol Pot. There was this one woman who told me fascism was an 'ecclesiastical belief'. Eventually I traced it back to something Guzman, their founder, had written: 'Fascism is an eclectic belief.' They just learn everything blindly by rote.' Yet they also had a lot of educated people in their ranks. 'At the University of Ayacucho where Guzman started the whole movement in the mid-seventies they all graduate to nothing. Sendero offers something, however misguided.' At the university Mark had asked why people join Sendero. They looked at him as if he was mad. 'This is supposed to be a place of rationality,' he argued. 'Get out of here before they hurt you,' a woman begged.

While more strident voices spoke of a country 'spiralling towards anarchy' or 'tearing itself apart', Mark saw Sendero's as a low-intensity revolution, a fuse burning slowly. A government general had summed up the situation recently: 'Sendero's not winning, but neither is the government.' One thing that was certain, though, was that both sides had guaranteed the aptness of the description 'Dirty War' for their mutual violence. As Amnesty International attested, the security forces gave as good as they got.

> During a search for 'disappeared' prisoners by Public Ministry investigators, a mass grave of at least fifty corpses, mostly those of young people, was found in Pucayacu, Ayacucho, in August 1984. The bodies showed signs of torture. The killers had tried to prevent identification by severing fingers and destroying their faces and clothing. Public prosecutors found grounds to charge with murder the naval officer commanding the Marine Infantry at Huanta, but the armed forces failed to produce him for trial. [Ayacucho, incidentally, is Quechua for 'corner of death'].

Mark thought Sendero would win, but not immediately. The day we spoke the Rodrigo Franco Right Wing Death Squad had hit back, killing the deputy from Puro, a left-winger called Edilberto Oroya. Things seemed to be hotting up.

'¿Qué te parece Peru, Mark?'

'Well, tell you one thing, I'm never bored here.'

III

Jim Leigh greeted me in the calm atmosphere of the Britanico Association of which he was the executive director. Mark Day had found an excitement in the present-day flux of Peru but I wanted to speak to someone whose happiness here had a longer root.

I had met Jim Leigh at a cocktail party given by the British Council during my first stay in Lima. On that warm evening clusters of Anglophiles stood in the green light of Justin Gilbert's garden taking drinks (pisco, gin, whisky) and snacks (prawn dips, avocado dips) from trays borne by small tuxedoed Indians. Those who carried the nibbles waited patiently with a plate for the detritus.

Justin was the associate director of the British Council in Lima. He had not long graduated from Cambridge and his face seemed to be engaged in a constant battle with itself – between the downward pull of class and position, which I liked to see as a mask, and a boyish smile which could not be quelled. He was an attentive host and introduced me to Jim Leigh, the railway engineer, and Jim Birbeck, the mining engineer. Both had given me glimpses of a Peru which was different from its present confusion. Though Jim Leigh had said to me when I called him on my return to Lima, 'Well, I don't know what I can tell you,' he had graciously agreed to speak to me.

Jim had come to Peru in 1946 to work for the Peruvian Corporation as engineer on the train line from Lima to Huancayo, the Central Railway of Peru, built out of guano profits by Henry Meiggs, 'The Yankee Pizarro'. He had spent his first five years, during which he had no leave, in Oroya in the highlands behind Lima. So what had been his first impressions of Peru?

'I was twenty-nine years old. I'd been an officer in the army for six and a half years. I had money in my pocket so I didn't give a shit.' The social life in Oroya had been good – 'hard drinking, hard playing' – and there were about seven hundred foreign nationals there, mostly involved in the mining industry.

'The mining companies tried to poach me but my heart was in the railway. Yes, I suppose it was the railway kept me in Peru. I mean it was a bit of a toy railway and with steam it was beautiful, beautiful. Beautiful . . .' He had sat on a cane chair at the back of his private carriage, inspecting the line with a drink in his hand. Pink gin had been his tipple.

There were still traces of the military about Jim Leigh. The erect bearing and impeccable dressing, the silver, groomed hair and the slightly upturned moustache were matched by a pleasing directness and a willing sense of humour. He admitted that he had kept mostly to his British friends all these years and he still had a distinct Lancashire accent. When he returned there now, he saw 'tremendous improvements' from the world he had known. 'I mean it's so much cleaner for one thing.' He noticed the reverse in Peru, in particular in Lima where after Oroya he had worked for twenty-five years.

'Old Lima was small, attractively so. Jiron de la Union – that was the main society street. It's the one that's – what do you call it now? *Pedestrianised*. Well, it used to have two or three tea-rooms and the girls and their mothers would walk up and down and we chaps in our boaters would proposition them. All the high-class shops were there. Now what's left? Welsch's, the jewellers.'

Once, it seems, Lima had been an elegant European city with its beach resort of Miraflores where city people went for the summer. Avenida Arequipa which united Miraflores and Lima itself was built by the English Railway in 1926. It was the end of the exclusivity of Miraflores as a rich Limēnos' summer residence, but it was a demise which enabled their descendants to see the suburbs of Miraflores, San Isidro and Barranco as *their* Lima, cut loose from the old collapsing centre. Jim Leigh saw it this way: 'Frankly, when I go downtown now, I find ninety-nine per cent of the people repulsive. They're dirty, they don't look happy – all they're interested in is survival.'

Since 1951, when he married a German girl whose parents owned a sugar hacienda up north, Jim had been settled in Peru. His four children 'love their Peru' and had refused his offer of sending them to university in Britain. And for himself, since the war had scattered most of his school friends and his sister was his only relation in Britain, he had never felt himself to be an exile.

'Till now,' he said, 'I've never spoken out against Peru. But now things really are getting out of hand. We're very much aware of it here where the number of students enrolling to study English over the last year or so has dropped from ten thousand to six. People just don't have the money.' The expat community too, which had sustained him, was getting thinner. The *Phoenix Phlasher*, the newsletter of the Phoenix Club, was calling for new members; as was the Lima Cricket Club where, with inflation out of control, the afternoon teas were growing more frugal.

'The Brits who are coming now,' Jim told me sadly, 'come for short-term contracts, just to do a technical job and then get out. Of course waves of expats left when General Velasco took power in 1968 in the left-wing military coup. Before then, foreigners were in charge of Peruvian labour but Velasco made them uppity and no one would dare tell them what to do.'

Still, the rot had set in even before Jim arrived in Peru. 'Before the Second World War, the upper-crust Peruvians were educated either at a British school or university. To the Peruvians the only civilised race in the world were the British.' Jim thought that the war was a split which had been decisive in breaking those close links between the two countries. But there had still been enough of the British in Peru to sustain him and to give him a happy life here.

'You should take that train to Huancayo, you know – at least a part of the way. That's what I tell everyone who comes here for a few days.' I told him that I might just do that, shook hands firmly and left the posters of thatched cottages and Buckingham Palace for the teeming traffic of Avenida Arequipa.

In Pursuit of Esther Williams
LIMA

I

'If you live in Lima, you can get used to misery and grime, you can go crazy or you can blow your brains out.' So says the narrator of Mario Vargas Llosa's apocalyptic novel about present day Peru, *The Real Life of Alejandro Mayta*. It had been a parting gift from the American photographer in La Paz and I had read it hungrily, drawn in by its power, but also because Vargas Llosa was on my 'interview list'.

'Mario Vargas Llosa has replaced Gabriel García Márquez as the South American novelist for gringos to catch up on,' trumpeted John Updike on the book cover. It was certainly not an accolade that would win him any new readers at home. For how could gringos appreciate the full ideological slant which many said warped his novels? And anyway, to many Peruvians, like Flavio the charango-player, was Vargas Llosa with his Knightsbridge apartment not halfway to being a gringo himself? 'What does he know of the life of the campesinos?' he had asked bitterly. 'He is hardly ever in Peru.'

Still, few readers free of ideological prejudice would argue that next to Gabriel García Márquez he is South America's leading novelist, establishing himself in that position with his first novel *The Time of the Hero* (1962), a excoriating satire on the military academy in Lima he had himself attended. Its impact was such that a thousand copies had been publicly burned. In the 1950s he had been a communist, in the 1960s a defender of the Cuban revolution and of leftist guerrillas in Peru.

'Peru is for me a kind of incurable disease,' he had once written, 'and my feeling for her is intense, bitter, and full of the violence that characterises passion.' Certainly Peru had given him subject matter Martin Amis would kill for; not just the images of decadence but the thing itself. Now Vargas Llosa was seeking to repay his debt. At the age of fifty-two, he headed the presidential challenge of

137

Libertad, the party which had formed around him when he had opposed what was seen as Alan Garcia's mammoth political gaffe of nationalising the country's banks. The once-communist now did not hide his admiration for Margaret Thatcher and her policies. A free market could save Peru from chaos and turn her into 'a country of property owners'.

In an interview for *Le Nouvel Observateur* that month, he argued for the restoration of the European part of Peruvian culture and life, 'because it is a way of being Peruvian'. He wanted Peru to be a European country, 'simply because it is the heir of Europe. It is not possible,' he continued, 'to be an exotic country. To accept this will be to admit that we will always be poor and ignorant, that we will never be able to profit from the contributions of civilisation, that we will never know modernity.'

Of three thousand years of Peruvian culture, only the last five hundred have involved Europe. So who was being addressed here? And more importantly, who was being ignored? Such political inequality explained the two hundred politicians assassinated in the last decade and the attempt to kill Vargas Llosa himself two months before.

The novelist in him who dealt with the complexity of Peruvian society and all its problems must have balked at the simple vision he had to present for his political campaign. Though there was a tradition of South American literary figures involving themselves in public life, surely Vargas Llosa's compromises were giving him pain. 'I am sacrificing my vocation, which is incompatible with politics. The conquest of power, power itself, is the negation of literary activity,' he declared.

The ex-President Fernando Belaunde Terry warned: 'Look you: Peru is not a guinea pig to experiment on or make jump through hoops' (*Expreso* – 24 April). But Vargas Llosa was on a crusade, and I was itching to interview him about it. However, every time I phoned, using our mutual friendship with Alastair Reid as a calling card, señor Vargas Llosa was in Arequipa; was in the USA; was very busy. Perhaps next week . . .

I set the phone back in its cradle and rested my trailing arm there as my eyes followed the white cable across the bare parquet floor of Alan's apartment and came to rest on the still eucalyptus trees beyond the barred windows. Lying on the settee in my underpants, once more I felt brushed by what Graham Greene called 'the wing of melancholia'. It is fed by the boredom felt by a traveller at rest, who must somehow animate the hours and days which threaten to wash over him. There is refuge in the trivial: 'I'll flick through Alan's small library again. There was a slim Anita Brookner there somewhere.' Or, 'Now where was that station that played the hits of the sixties?' Finding either, I could boil up some water once more in the tin lid that needed the tin opener to lift it, and have another cup of coffee . . .

To lose that kicking-my-heels feeling as I waited for my 'scoop' with Vargas Llosa, I took a colectivo down Arequipa towards 'the misery and grime' of downtown Lima. Hunched in the back of a battered van, a trickle of sweat down my chest, I watched as the teenage conductor hopped in and out, ran alongside the van at the lights, whistled at prospective passengers and bawled out his route: 'Eh Lima! Lima! Lima! Tacna! Tacna! Tacna!' I thought of all the people here working at jobs so basic they could never improve – excepting the bravado in this case of jumping on and off at some speed – jobs that did not even have the adult dignity of being closed to children. There is no age barrier for the shoeshiner.

The huge monastery of San Francisco was showing an exhibition of art from the period of the viceroys: *Pintura en el Virreinato del Peru*. In one of the roomfuls of theatrical, joyless religious works, many gloomy, sadistic oils, four walls of severed, bruise-blue heads stared at each other and the bloody plates on which they sat. In contrast, the courtyard was bright and airy, the rooms themselves palatial. This was seventeenth-century Lima, imperial and European.

A stone's throw from the monastery was the Desamparados Station, its arches and colonnades topped by a grand, mantelpiece clock, from where I would be catching the train to Huancayo. And next to it stood the government palace with MPs in white helmets and camouflage gear making sure pedestrians kept to the path marked out for them. Armed to the hilt and in reflective sunglasses, they were determinedly unsmiling. These were no friendly traffic cops.

I crossed the River Rimac into the district of that name. The river was mud-brown and flowed swiftly around scrubby islands of grey rubble. When I lifted my eyes I saw the dry hills which back Lima with their sprawling shanty housing, and of course the Cross.

A little way down the street, where Trujillo met Avenida Francisco Pizarro, was a small plaza, the focal point of which was a blue, flaking church. In the middle of the plaza was a dry well with an iron lamp-standard flowering over it. From such details – the yellow façades in a state of collapse, the broken, wooden balconies over dirty, dismal shops – it was still possible to excavate the charm old Lima must have had. But it did demand an effort of the imagination greater than in any of Europe's *vieux quartiers*; an effort that was encouraged nowhere beyond the immediate centre.

Beneath iron lamps jutting out from the walls on Trujillo, past the empty Teatro Perricholi – 'Hoy SAH . . . R' was the billing – doors opened on to dark alleyways full of suspicion; miserable people with gaunt faces hunkered on the streets. Even the presidential candidate, whose prospective home (the presidential palace) was only two minutes from this downbeat scene, had described the city's prospects with an unremitting bleakness. These are the last words of *The Real Life of Alejandro Mayta*: 'A year ago I began to concoct this story the same way I'm ending it, by speaking about the garbage that's invading every neighbourhood in the capital of Peru.'

Back at the Plaza de Armas in Café Haiti, 'Your Restaurant Friend' as it advertised itself, I looked through the glass portals at the statue of the mounted Francisco Pizarro, founder of this, the City of Kings. Down narrow streets into the hazy distance stretched the elegant balconies. (With a bit of imagination . . .) Yet a few blocks away from this neat grid were the heaving lengths of Abancay, of Garcilaso de la Vega with their rows of cobblers and machine-part booths and old magazine and bottle stalls, all their 'cottage industries', crowding the pavements. These were some of *los informales*: poor operators in the informal economy who made up about half of Peru's workforce; the 'entrepreneurs' to whom Vargas Llosa hoped he would appeal.

Sipping my coffee, I mused that the past here was a past beyond elegy; the pressures of the present were too heavy and too insistent to give breath to such a form. Nor was there the acceptance of the past that an elegy acknowledges. Rather there seemed to be a fiercely partisan and divisive nostalgia: held by Sendero for a pre-colonial, equable peasant society; by Vargas Llosa for the European milieu in which he felt comfortable; held in smaller measure by Jim Leigh for a Lima that was manageable and respectful.

Again it was an emotion with which I could sympathise, remembering the crow in Liz Lochhead's play, *Mary Queen of Scots Got Her Head Chopped Off*: 'National flower: the thistle. National pastime: nostalgia.' But this Peruvian strain of nostalgia seemed to invite the most simple solutions, back to year dot or back to Europe, in which the spraying of a valley with the defoliant SPIKE was not out of keeping. Dangerous when it seemed to me everything in Peru demanded the most constructive effort of the imagination, even seeing. Jim Leigh's Jiron de la Union was a case in point. I took a walk down it again on my way to visit Carlos German Belli, poet and journalist.

It was hard to see now how the Jiron de la Union had once been. I thought of Edinburgh's Princes Street as my parents described it before the war: an elegant social and shopping street 'before the chainstores ruined it'. The Jiron de la Union, a narrow street, must have retained its status, like London's Bond Street, through the exclusivity of its shops. Now it was seething with people selling everything from sanitary towels to white mice in paper bags. There was a strong strolling police presence, but still it was not a relaxed street.

Casa Welsch, the upmarket jeweller's, stood on a corner. I entered through its copper-beaten, art deco inner doors into a dark, oppressive space. Grey, wooden panelling dimmed the spirit further. The glass cases seemed more appropriate to a museum, and a sharp-eyed curator followed me around looking disgruntled, as if the times had cheated him.

Carlos German Belli worked as an essayist on *Suplemento Dominical*, the literary supplement of *El Comercio*. The *Comercio* building was on the corner of Jiron Miroquesada, two blocks from the Jiron de la Union. This was real downtown Lima; business Lima: banks, good policing, minimum hawkers, a big-windowed café called the City. The *Comercio* building had heavy brass fittings on the doors, a spacious marble atrium with black diamonds set in the floor, a stained-glass roof, classical detail. Such buildings, and there were many in central Lima, were a shock to enter, so often were they surrounded by dirt, litter, grime and the ubiquitous money-changers.

I was guided through a series of dark corridors to Carlos's office. He was a slightly built man, bald, with bright, lively eyes: the eyes of an optimist. We talked about Alastair Reid who had suggested I visit him ('Ah, Aleesterr. ¿Como esta Aleesterr?') and then about the national obsession with Peruvian identity.

'This country is going through a process of integration,' he maintained, 'integration of all the races and traditions who live here. It is not only a problem of Peru, but of Latin America as a whole. Of course it is not a problem that will be solved immediately. It will take twenty years or so, but yes, I am optimistic that the situation will resolve itself.' He smiled a polite full-stop, so I asked him whether he tried to embrace the political and social upheaval in his poetry.

'No, for me there is only the word. I must just try to write as well as I can.' We agreed it was the poet's only duty.

He smiled again. Our meeting had been at eleven: it was now midday. It took a few moments' more silence before I realised this had definitely not been an invitation for an early lunch. With galloping inflation, professional people lived in 'reduced circumstances' and no one had any money for the mythically long lunches I associate with journalism. Nor did I feel our meeting such a success that he would want to prolong it if I offered to take him out. Perhaps I had come too hungry for answers, and had sat too close to the edge of my chair. Perhaps I should have limited myself to poetry and the passing on of a friend's regards.

I had read one of his articles for *El Comercio* titled 'Lima from the Outside', which was written around the persistent aptness of the phrase 'Lima la horrible', coined by Cesar Moro in 1949. Perhaps he was tired of views from the outside. Clumsily, I said I had better leave him to get on with his work. Smiling, and I think a touch relieved, he agreed.

II

I'm getting out
& going some 30 kilometres towards the coast
where one day I saw tall dark grass
reaching to the sea,　　　& my only joy
will be that grass brushing my ears,
my only comfort those easy waters,
I'll just stretch out on the wet sand, shoeless,
close my eyes,　　　& shut my heart
like the saltwater snails,
the hard red ones.

It was almost twenty years since I had been captivated by the poetry of Antonio Cisneros. When I was a student at St Andrews I used to go in every day to Henderson's bookshop, pull from the shelves *The Spider Hangs Too Far From The Ground* and read a few of the poems before I could afford the sixteen shillings it cost. His image on the back cover was dark-eyed, intense; very handsome. Below, it announced, 'Antonio Cisneros, born in Lima in 1942, is one of the most exciting young poets writing in Latin America today. His poems combine a deep involvement with Peru and its history with a fine control of language and structure. The result is an amazing freshness, intensity and precision.' It was as far as I can remember the first Latin American writing I had come across.

The book contained longer meditations ('Chronicles') set in London and Paris, but the ones that excited me were the short lyrics with all these mysterious, beautiful names: Paracas, Pachacamac, Atacama, Tupac Amaru, Ayacucho, Tarma. The poems themselves slipped down like good ceviche – fresh, tangy and memorable. In fact the ending of the above poem, with its definitive closure, has remained one of my favourite endings to a poem and one I have inadvertently (?) echoed.

Now the poet in person leant over the balcony of his house in Miraflores to tell me in English that someone was coming to let me in. For the second day running the air in Lima had been unusually clear. 'What a blue sky for Lima,' I called up.

'Yes, it's like a different city. Better,' he laughed. I found out later he did not consider himself a Limeño at all: Miraflores was his town: leafy, open, beside the sea. 'We were on our own till 1929 and still we talk about "going to Lima". This is my town. I was born just two houses away.'

The apartment was top-floor, washed by sunny light. The walls, rich with original drawings, paintings and photographs, the packed bookshelves, reflected the interests of someone who had been a recognised poet on the international scene for many years. 'I am a cosmopolitan man. If I am in Hungary, I don't say, "Oh, I must eat ceviche; how I miss pisco." '

He was also a man of the Left and one-time friend of Vargas Llosa with whom he had shared a flat in London. But he had broken with Vargas Llosa ten years ago because he could not bear his political views. '*The Real Life of Alejandro Mayta*? Yes, it's the same as *The*

War at the End of the World: designed to show that anyone who holds any ideology is wrong.'

We talked about London in the sixties where he had gone to live after winning a scholarship to study in Paris. 'Well, London in the sixties was where it was happening.' And about . . . 'Ah, yes, Alastair Reid, the guy who lived on a houseboat. Ah yes, yes. I've had better times in my life than now.'

'Better?'

'Oh yes, much better.'

Antonio was now forty-six, his eyes heavily lined, but with thick, wavy, grey hair and a tall, rangy body; still a very attractive man. He was dressed in a light blue, open-necked shirt and cords and moved in a relaxed, languid way from easy-chair to kitchen to bring us yet another beer. He sat cross-legged and when he exhaled his cigarette smoke, his mouth opened wide and he showed his beautiful feline, pink tongue, letting the smoke spiral slowly upwards, an echo of the elegant and dramatic gestures he made constantly with his fine hands as he talked.

'Yes, viveza. Well you know, it always goes along with criolla. Viveza criolla. Los vivos were the people who came down with Simon Bolivar. They considered themselves better, smarter than those who came from Europe. They were Americans, but Spanish-Americans. So los vivos lived in cities, white cities remember, and ripped off the Andeans who came down from the mountains. There's an old story of how one sells off the Plaza San Martin to a campesino. "*Qué bonita*," says the campesino. "Eh, eh, you like? You wanna buy?"' Antonio, the storyteller, put on a wheeler-dealer's voice, '"Yours for a hundred pesetas."'

When his wife Negra arrived, Antonio folded her arm in place round his neck, laughing like an innocent youth. But his natural insouciance was clouded by tiredness and worry, as his enthusiasm ('Yes, I'm going to write an article about socialism – what is there to be ashamed of? – and I'm going to dedicate it to you.') was frayed.

He was tired working as a professor of French at the University of San Marcos and as an editor of a cultural weekly to support his family and he was worried about their future. 'I'd like to leave Peru for a few years. I want something better for my children.'

To Antonio, Peru was going through something now it should have experienced five hundred years ago, or certainly at the start of this century. He cited Mexico as an example of what he meant: a country that had its revolution in 1910 and since then had remained a similar country in an institutional sense to the one that had been established then. Peru had never had its revolution and yet it had great injustices, both social and political.

'There's a historical debt to pay,' he said with bitterness. 'We're not the guilty ones, but we're being asked to pay. I just wish it wasn't happening now, in my time, with my son, with my daughters. Why not years ago or in three centuries' time? No, Carlos Belli is an excellent poet, but he is naïve about politics. He is right to the extent that Latin America is one country. Make no mistake about that. Abroad you meet a Latin, no matter which country, you're brothers.' I imagined the young Antonio embracing his Latin brothers in the pubs of Notting Hill and Camden Town. I thought he too might be there, before his face darkened. 'But in this, he is wrong. This is a time of disintegration, not integration.'

We talked about all the book titles I had culled – *Peru – Problems and Possibilities* – titles that saw Peru as an adolescent country with severe growing pains. Antonio's sadness at his country's plight was compounded by deep awareness of Peruvian history. 'It is a mistake to think of us as just a young country. We are older than Italy, older than Germany, yes? And, as an ancient civilisation, older than most countries in the world. We may be poor now, but we have been rich. Very rich. But now . . . Now, we have no money. I have no money. Last year, we had twenty per cent more than we needed to live. Now each month we have forty per cent less. This beer is on tick from an understanding shopkeeper.

'And another deficit about this country nowadays' – I was aware of Antonio's need, once started, to spit it all out – 'you know, I travel a lot and the Peruvian is one of the worst passports in the world to travel with. The Peruvian and the Colombian. Everything you have must come out. Sometimes, I get annoyed, but then I think it's silly. I mean we grow ninety per cent of the world's cocaine: it's natural they're going to check.'

As a socialist his despondency and pessimism were compounded by the belief that everything, including nationalisation, had been tried in Peru: there were no big haciendas anymore. And he saw Peru as a country that had never been very nationalistic, not like Mexico or Argentina or Chile, but a country that had strong democratic impulses. 'You can see it in all the newspapers and magazines that are published here. Sixteen daily papers. Sixteen! Ah, not only do we have to suffer our collapse, we have to read about it all the time! And you can see it in these hideous grey school uniforms.' Grinning, he pointed to Soledad, his fourteen-year-old daughter who had just arrived home from school. 'Everyone in Peru, no matter what the school, must wear the same.'

So, I wondered, did people join Sendero because all else had failed?

'No, they join because of fear. Sendero are what? Fifty thousand at the most. And many of them fourteen or fifteen years old. But they have guns, so people are afraid.' As we talked, somewhere on the outskirts of Jauja, central Peru, sixty-two Senderos and six military personnel were dying in a pitched battle. The next day, *Expreso* carried the headline 'Viernes Sangriento'. Bloody Friday.

And why did Vargas Llosa want to go into politics?

'To be President of Peru. Like being an admiral in the Bolivian navy!' Antonio laughed.

By the time we climbed into his Volkswagen Beetle, apart from a break for a late lunch of shellfish soup and fresh white fish and rice ('We have no heart disease with this diet'), we had been drinking the pilsen-type beer steadily for six hours. Antonio was going up to Barranco to give a reading and was full of good spirits, no hint of cloudy mood swings, as we drove along the shore road of Malecon.

'This is my town. Look! Over there, my nearest neighbour is China. Think about that. You know, we exist too. We on the coast; we have a right to be here too.'

'You love this place, don't you, in spite of everything?'

'Yes, as you love your place. It's like I love my mother, but I can't say she's young and beautiful any more.' He continued over my laughter, 'Ah yes, poets must deal with reality. Novelists with fiction.'

We embraced in the small car and I spilled out into the dusky light of Avenida Armendariz.

III

I took a few deep breaths, something you don't often do in Lima, and negotiated my way through the traffic hurtling along Armendariz. Jim Birbeck lived on the other side of the road in a large, comfortable villa filled with antique furniture, paintings and mementos from his and his wife's prestigious backgrounds. As we waited for her to appear, he showed me round a few rooms, honey-light on polished wood, pleased at my interest in his collection of paintings. There were sombre religious paintings, including a striking madonna and child ('school of the school of Cuzco sort of thing'), pleasant landscapes and portraits of eminent Peruvians. He pointed to the portrait of a beautiful woman looking over her shoulder in a haughty way.

'That's probably the most valuable painting we have,' he said. 'Dieguez painted it of Rosana when she was still his student.'

'Ah, then your wife is an artist?'

'No, she didn't think she was good enough and gave it up.'

'Were you courting her when this painting was being done?'

'Yes, I was.'

'Well she doesn't look as if she'd make it too easy for you!'

'Exactly. She was from a very important family in its time – private armies and all that. And Dieguez said he wanted to capture some of that past in her.'

Round the walls of the dining-room were hand-finished prints of North American Indians by George Catlin. 'Terrible, you know, he couldn't find a publisher for a book of these in America. The two volumes were published in England in 1841.' I was leafing through these 1841 editions when Señora Birbeck made her entrance. She was smaller than I expected, almost bird-like, and had no trace of the hauteur of her portrait. Rather she was solicitous and determined everything should be right: the pisco sour should have been frothier; the nuts should have had raisins.

Jim Birbeck himself was a slight figure in his early sixties, a little stooped, but relaxed and sincere and with an animating intelligence. Below his thin, scraped hair, his greygreen eyes shone like a cat's. 'Just help yourself now. Don't worry about me,' he advised as I made very heavy weather levering myself out of a sofa to pass some nuts across the large coffee table between us. I had phoned him to talk about his experiences in Peru and why the country had held him for so long. He had told me he would be delighted to meet me again; to come for drinks this evening.

His story. He had a Peruvian friend at the Royal School of Mines, part of London University, who had written and told him there was a job in Peru. To cut a long story short, as he put it himself, he became the first non-Harvard geologist working for an American company based in Sierra de Vasca. He was six years there, by which time he had made his commitment to Rosana and to Peru; then seven years with a Canadian company based in Lima. In 1960 he had set up on his own as a consultant and a few years later set up his own mining company with Peruvian friends, opening lead, zinc, silver and copper mines. However, with falling prices, rising interest rates and an expansionist programme, they had run into problems and between 1981 and 1983 had had to shut down three mines and pay off seven hundred men. He hoped to open a gold mine in the jungle next year, to get all the mines working successfully and to be in a better position should he decide to sell.

This I would have thought was enough to be getting on with, but Jim Birbeck – like Barry, like Toni, like Mark – was fuelled with a restless energy: a snake that turned and twisted. To keep sane, he said, he needed sidelines. 'I'm not the sort of person just to go into the office and that's all.' He was vice-chairman of the Asociacion Cultural Peruano-Britanica and head of its cultural sub-committee and he had recently become involved in starting a non-profit-making association for Maria Reich's affairs in Nazca. ('Maria has friends all over the world because of the Lines,' Jim told me when I suggested that it seemed a pretty lonely way to spend a life.) These two activities, I ventured, seemed to reflect the two sides of Jim Birbeck, the English and the Peruvian.

'Yes,' he admitted, 'I'm an ancestor worshipper. One of the motives for coming to Peru was economic. I'd thought to pull the family back up to where it had been.' His tales of being taken round Dorset pubs with Augustus John, a friend of the family, when he was a fifteen-year-old schoolboy at Winchester sounded like the apogee of a quintessentially English rite of passage. His father later married one of John's models, Chicita. Jim had retained his roots in England and had a son living in London. 'In fact I could be quite comfortably settled in London tomorrow.'

However, he had not lived the rather closed life of the expatriate in Peru. His friendships and his activities had been with the people of the country. 'One's interested in one's interests,' as he put it, 'and most of the expats aren't interested in my interests.'

'What are your interests?' I asked.

'The human race.'

One of his motives for coming to Peru had been economic, but the other had been 'intellectual curiosity – going into something really profound in terms of human history'. But what, I wondered, was the Peru like that he found when he came here, when he met Jim Leigh, all these years ago?

'Peru? It was an organised country which could be called a civilised country. Everyone was in their place. A peasant was a peasant; an oligarchy an oligarchy; a politician a politician. And by and large everyone was satisfied. The problems of course were latent: masses of people living as they did six hundred years ago, great gaps between wealth and poverty, a limited form of democracy.'

'So change doesn't surprise you?'

'No, it was inevitable. What disappoints is that the changes were organised by theoretical socialists; that the only progressive banner was the socialist banner.'

Moreover, Jim Birbeck had seen himself as an agent of change because of his involvement with mining. 'Mines mean roads and a road changes everything. There's a delicate human ecology in the mountains and in mountain areas. Yes, people got damaged.'

It was a sign of Jim's empathy with the country that this was not something said lightly or without sadness. For after the first six years he had fallen in love with the country; the contrast between past and present, the natural contrasts, the differing climates. 'I found myself in sympathy with the nature of the country. Mountains make me happy. I respect the feelings of mountains, rocks and animals, because they feel these things in others.' To illustrate his point he told me the story of how once, when he was in the mountains with another geologist, an old man had said, 'The mountains don't like this person. It would be better for him not to go up there.' Immediately afterwards it had begun to snow heavily. Listening to Jim's cultured, softly rounded vowels, it was strange to be put in mind of Ricardo Quispe Mamani with whom he shared the same simple statement of experience. I told Jim about los Hinteles.

'Actually, it's los *Gentiles* and a common belief. They have it for anything they don't understand or can't explain, in the way that people once did with Stonehenge.' This was the Jim Birbeck I warmed to, the one who had ridden a pack horse through the Andes, listening to the campesinos and the Indians, respecting their tales and beliefs; the one who I felt had left much of the weight of his past trussed up in some smoky gentlemen's club in London to come to a place where it could not come between him and his interest in ordinary people.

His political heart too was a mix of popular sympathy and traditional values. He was desperately saddened by the present state of Peru but he had faith in the people. He fetched me a copy of *El Otro Sendero* (The Other Sendero) by Hernando de Soto, a bestselling study of 'the informal economy'. 'The conclusion is,' he told me, 'that the official government has nothing to do with the real impulse of the people which is towards private enterprise. These people should be given maximum opportunity. Instead bureaucracy gets worse and worse and the people get more desperate.'

It was the only time frustration breached, slightly, his aristocratic calm. For my part 'the informal economy' dignified what was the people's impulse to survive, to scrabble a living any way possible short of begging, in a crippled and corrupt Third World economy. It was not socialism after all which had created the shanty-towns, Los Pueblos Jovenes: *El Otro Sendero*, it seemed, absolved capitalism of any responsibility whatsoever.

'The history of Peru in the last twenty-five years is a textbook example,' he gave me as his last words, 'of how theoretical socialism can ruin a prosperous country. But I'm still hopeful in the next five to ten years of seeing a remarkable recovery. The people are solid and sensible; they won't put up with Sendero imposing on them for much longer.'

I downed one more pisco sour and thanked Jim for his time and his interest, and Señora Birbeck for her forebearance. Then, feeling expansive in the night, in a mood to toast poets and poetry, I took a taxi to Barranco where I walked into a couple of bars to be told I'd just missed Antonio. Thus, the sensible gods being with me, my day fizzled gently to a close.

IV

I returned to Barranco the next day to meet Claudia Izaguirre Godoy, a journalist who had been with a group at Tambopata when I was there. I had only spoken to her briefly at the airport at Puerto Maldonaldo as we waited for the flight back to Cuzco. 'Yes, we all heard about your robbery. We are very sad for you, but what can you say?' Still, she had given me her number in Lima and told me to call her if she could be of any help.

'Barranco is the most artistic and romantic district in Lima,' she informed me now in her rather clipped, dogmatic English. It enjoyed a reputation as Lima's Greenwich Village and at night it had that light, airy atmosphere of being part of a spontaneous musical that Latin America can give. Even the foreboding atmosphere outside the Ormeño bus station in downtown Lima in the early morning was transformed when its metal doors opened, and suddenly it was: lights! music! action! To brassy beat music, the vendors, the shoeshiners, the taxi-taxi-taxi, chiclet-chiclet, paper sellers moved amongst the passengers shouting their custom. It was a scene that appeared almost to be choreographed.

The excitement was more so on an evening in Barranco. When downtown Lima was at its most threatening, its daytime hubs abandoned, its narrow streets dark and urinous, where 'no one, mister, remember is your friend', Barranco exuded a positively sexual charge as couples and loosely knitted groups milled between bars, restaurants and live music. This was life turned inside out, lived communally. My first evening in Barranco, soon after arriving in Lima, I was borne along by its energy. The largely student crowd, pursuing pleasure, had ignored the gringo in their midst. I remembered Alastair Reid telling me about his 'South American self' as we ran to find shelter from the rain to watch the firework display at the Edinburgh Festival. Barranco was as close as I got to the image I had then: one-dimensional, loud, emotional, colourful – *Flying Down To Rio*.

Now in daylight Barranco had a faded elegance, almost the feel of a Victorian seaside resort with its bandstand centrepiece. Claudia and I walked down a path until we reached a view over the coast. We looked along the rubble of the eroded cliff face, the livid trees that seemed to have been caught in an avalanche and their growth smothered. The distant buildings of Miraflores and Callao were grey in the misty fug that hung over Lima. El Oceano Pacifico. It was so bleak it was difficult to know what to say.

Claudia led me into a restaurant called La Ermita where we were only the second table of diners. Everything was immaculately starched from table linen to waiter. I glanced over the menu and almost laughed out loud at prices five times higher than anywhere I had been. Even though I had changed money that morning, inflation was so pacy one changed only thirty or forty dollars at one time and I knew this was going to be tight. But Claudia, though only twenty-six, was a serious companion and regarded my smilingly raised eyebrows uneasily.

She worked as a journalist on *El Comercio* which was also paying her through a law course. She loved her job but said that there was an uneasy feeling among political journalists at the moment. *El Comercio* had staked its support behind Vargas Llosa. 'But no one knows what is going to happen. No one will vote for APRA again,' Claudia explained, 'and the Left is in disarray. But Vargas Llosa has not much of a political profile here. The image-makers are really having to work hard on him.' I smiled at the irony of Vargas Llosa himself being turned into a fiction to win over those campesinos who had never seen him and could not read him.

The meal, corvina (sea-bass), was delicious but as I had expected I did not have enough intis to pay for it and they would not accept dollars. I assumed this rebuttal of what everyone else was desperate for was a sign of class.

'I'm sorry, Claudia,' I started, 'I was going to buy you lunch but they won't take dollars.'

'Then pay in intis.'

'I don't have enough'

'But haven't you got a *card*?'

I heard a distant echo of Petra. 'No.'

Amazement in her big, dark eyes. Claudia spoke to the waiter and eventually he agreed to accept my dollars. That Claudia had made no move to share some of the cost did not come as any great surprise to me. This was another coastal phenomenon according to Mark: the other side of machismo. 'Okay,' the airhead logic went, 'you can be like that but you're going to have to pay for it.' Even someone as intelligent and ambitious as Claudia could not shake off such social assumptions, so in the colectivo back to Miraflores it already felt the most natural thing that I pay for us both. It was a paltry amount so I write this not out of any sense of pique, but to illustrate one more facet of Limeño life and one more reason why I felt it was getting near time to take a break from a city that was as enervating to live in as it was strangely compelling.

There was even less to hold me when I was finally told the next day that I had no interview with Vargas Llosa. His secretary told me, 'Señor Vargas Llosa and I looked over his schedule to try and find a small space and you know it's impossible, just impossible. You haven't been lucky in your timing. He was around the country, then in New York and next week he goes to Europe.' Ay. Ay. Ay. In

Samaná I had read his wonderfully inventive novel *Aunt Julia and the Scriptwriter*, reputedly based on his courting and first marriage to his aunt. The ending of that novel was somewhat soured for me by his curt dismissal of the relationship as a stage in his life he had jettisoned. *Aunt Julia Replies* had been the lady's riposte and a bestseller in Peru. Now Vargas Llosa was married to his cousin. Over the months I had created a fiction of the man in my head – stiff, distant, calculating. Had Manuel Puig not designated him in his Hollywood pantheon as Esther Williams? 'Oh so disciplined!' In a poem called 'Where Truth Lies' Alastair Reid had written, 'what is true/lies between you and the idea of you.' Now I only had the energy and power of the novels and the ambivalent messages of reportage to go on. *Lamentablamente*, the man himself could not disturb my reading of him.[1]

[1]In the first round of the presidential elections in April 1990, Vargas Llosa secured only thirty-five per cent of the vote and not the forty-five per cent expected, while Alberto Fujimori, a former university rector of direct Japanese descent, came from nowhere to secure twenty-eight per cent for the Centre-Right. In the second round at the end of May, Alberto Fujimori defeated the right-wing candidature of Mario Vargas Llosa.

Vargas Llosa's own fascinating account of his political odyssey can be read in *Granta 36: Vargas Llosa for President*.

PART FOUR

Peru to the bitter end

A Trip into Peru Profundo
SAN PEDRO DE CASTA

I

When I had discussed the apparent lack of a unified Peruvian identity with the poet and critic Washington Delgado in his book-lined study in Lince, a district on the downmarket side of Miraflores, he had observed, 'In Peru there's also the split between el campo y la ciudad, the country and the town. Now in Europe there's not that split. In Europe, in both you expect running water, services etc, yes? Here in Peru, no. They're two completely different worlds.'

In Lima the two worlds had met: it had become a refugee city. Once city life had been the attraction for the rural population but now fear was filling the coastal cities and towns – Lima, Pisco, Arequipa. Fear and, as Ramon Ochoa, the agricultural expert at Action Aid spelled out to me, long-term agricultural failures in the Andes themselves.

During the Inca period the land had supported ten million people. During the viceroy period this had fallen to four million. The prime land, the fifty-two coastal valleys, was taken by the large haciendas and the native Peruvians pushed into the mountains. In 1969, the military government, working with agrarian reform movements, had implemented the Restitution of Grandes Tierras to small farmers and cooperatives, but the cooperative movement had suffered from changes of direction in government and chronic underfunding.

'The statistics relating to potato yields are instructive here,' Ramon told me. 'In Europe the yield is sixty thousand kilos per hectare; in the coastal valleys of Peru forty thousand; in the Andes, with no technology, it's four thousand. If there is sufficient water the production in the Andes is good. If not, not very good at all.' Or, as Ricardo had said about Amantani, 'Without rain, triste la vida aquí.'

'The Incas had elaborate irrigation systems,' Ramon continued, 'and they knew about crop rotation. In many places now, the soil is exhausted and in need of fertiliser, but fertiliser is expensive and so the problem gets worse. In the jungle where many of those displaced from the Andes go, the situation is even more severe. Land there is very poor. It needs a twenty-year rotation cycle. Of course the natives know this but not the slash-and-burn farmers.'

I was anxious to learn what Action Aid was doing about the problem and also keen for a restorative trip into what is known as 'Peru profundo'. As a character tells Alejandro Mayta, 'The real Peru [is] in the mountains and not along the coast, among the Indians and the condors and the peaks of the Andes, not here in Lima, a foreign, lazy, anti-Peruvian city, because from the time the Spaniards had founded it, it had looked towards Europe and the United States and turned its back on Peru.'

II

Toni arranged a weekend trip for me to San Pedro de Casta and Ingeniero (engineer) Luca Mazon picked me up from Alan's flat at seven one Friday morning. In the early haze, which may never have lifted, we passed a park where there was a winding queue a hundred yards long. 'For rice,' Luca informed me. We collected the other members of the project, Miguel Remigio Marigualu (ingeniero agronomo) and Abraham Diaz (ingeniero zootecnista), straightened up and headed for Chosica about twenty-five kilometres from Lima. Once a summer town favoured by Lima's aristocracy, the rich agricultural land between itself and the city had been killed by chemicals and now only houses grew there: dusty, dispiriting settlements.

'Lima now has one-third of Peru's population,' Luca told me. 'People from the Andes think they're better off in the city, but the difference between Lima and San Pedro de Casta is like the difference between the earth and the moon. The aim of the project is to keep people in the Andes.'

Before we reached Chosica we passed through the curtain of Limeño mist and into strong sunshine. At Chosica we breakfasted quickly on coffee and fried egg rolls before Señor Mazon waved us off on our snub-nosed bus, smiling like a grey-haired uncle. As we began the slow climb to San Pedro, I asked Abraham about his involvement in the project.

'In the Andes there is not much meat and because of that there is much illness. The criollos don't have the resistance to altitude that the Incas had. We are reintroducing animals that the Incas used to have – partridge, guinea pig and alpaca. Alpaca is a very rich source of protein. One kilo of alpaca is equal to two kilos of beef in terms of protein.'

As Abraham talked, the driver was having an animated conversation with a young pigtailed girl at his side. I looked over spectacular drops to the Rio Santa Eulalia which the dirt road skirted with breathtaking precision. We were climbing into the heart of Peru, the great Andean cordillera, caused by the buckling of the earth's crust; climbing from six hundred metres to three thousand in just sixty kilometres. All enjoyed my gasps, my incredulity. I hoped these buses would have the benefit of a ground crew like an aircraft, but knew it was just one driver who knew the cranky ways of his engine.

Miguel tapped my shoulder and pointed. 'These trees. Way up there. *Arriba*,' rolling his Rs like a waterfall, 'San Pedro de Casta.' I bent my head to crane up at a mountain-top with a few bristles of trees. It seemed an unlikely spot to build; an impression confirmed by my first sighting of the shape of the village. If a stretch of land could be compared to a hand on which a snooker cue might rest, then San Pedro de Casta sat between the pronounced wrist-bone and the pinky-knuckle; but to complete the image, the outstretched fingers forming the sheer mountainside would have to be at least three times their normal length.

We got off the bus where a deep valley divided us from the town, and scrambled down a dry earth path to the project on the hillside of Casagayan. The community, the modern version of the Inca organisation of the ayllu, worked here each weekend. On the way down to the simple wooden hut which was the social centre of all the activity, we passed a chain of water-carriers all saying a muffled 'Buenas tardes.'

The project itself was spread over half a square mile on ground which obeyed the first principle of the Andes: if there is land where you can stand without falling over, then that is land you can plant. Here, fast-growing eucalyptus trees had been planted at intervals to hold the soil together and furrows curved to retain water. What was grown was decided by the whole community with advice from the project team: potatoes, wheat, onions, cabbages; all grown without chemical help. Abraham crouched over a large tank sunk into the ground and flicked his fingers through the water: eight carp were slowly growing here. If they were a success more would be bred.

We watched Faustino Dhivores, the local project chief, a slow, thoughtful man in his fifties whom Millet might have engraved, dig up potatoes using the metal crow-bar with its chisel end that was needed to work the dry earth (the Incas' tool was similar, only made of wood). Two young boys helping him loaded their smocks like aprons and we followed them to the hut for a late lunch. There, before my ears burst into flame, I sought sanctuary from the sun.

Four girls had been stoking with brushwood an oven built with a low wall of stones and a dome of clods of baked earth. With the many air holes the fire burned fiercely. When the clods were thought hot enough the fire was allowed to die, the ashes raked out, the potatoes thrown in and a few clods collapsed on top of them: more potatoes, more clods. When the lot had been collapsed the oven was covered with earth and the baking potatoes left for about twenty minutes. In the shade of the hut I asked Abraham what the government did to help agriculture.

'Nothing.'

'Nothing?'

'No. Nothing at all. The government favours the consumer more than the producer. It doesn't allow for transport costs and such to the producer. And there is much money given to agriculture by other agencies that is lost in bureaucracy – the agriculturists stay in Lima; they don't know the land.'

Later, in the spartan room in the village with its bunk beds and assortment of veterinary and musical instruments, I would see posters about the cultivation of la tuna (cactus), about keeping el cuy (guinea pig), about making a compost heap and an oven of bricks. The posters were produced by three agencies: el Centro de Investigacion y Capacitacion Campesina (CICCA), el Instituto de Desarrollo y Medio Ambientc (IDMA), and el Servicio Evangelico Peruano de Accion Social (SEPAS). Grand titles and acronyms all, but none of them, Miguel told me, received government money. Nor did the agencies where Miguel and Abraham worked the other four days of their seven-day week. ('You need two jobs to live,' said Miguel, at thirty-nine father of two college-age children. 'But it's sad to have no time for your family.') Much of the money for such agencies and for this Action Aid project came from the EC.

'The agriculturalists don't understand the land,' Abraham continued, 'and neither do the teachers who come here. Good teachers don't want to come and live here. So they get the fourth-grade ones who know nothing of agriculture or the history of this area. They try to teach the children about the Second World War and inapplicable maths.' The children, as they say, vote with their feet and Peru lives with an illiteracy rate of between forty and fifty per cent.

Faustino raked out a potato, broke it open and declared it ready. He handed it to me while the girls began raking out the others with occasional 'yows!' and hand-shakings when they brushed against a hot clod. The potatoes were thrown on a sack to cool and a whole white cheese slapped on to a plate.

'Take them together; the cheese is good with the potato,' Abraham advised.

'Could do with one more week to mature,' said Miguel, savouring the creamy cheese.

> They say that we do not know anything
> That we are backwardness
> That our heads need changing for a better one
> They say that some learned men are saying this about us
> These academics who reproduce themselves
> In our own lives
> What is there on the banks of these rivers, Doctor?
> Take out your binoculars
> And your spectacles
> Look if you can.
> Five hundred flowers
> From five hundred different types of potato
> Grow on the terraces
> Above abysses
> That your eyes don't reach
> Those five hundred flowers
> Are my brain
> My flesh

The poem, 'A Call To Certain Academics' by Jose Maria Arguedas, one of the few writers to choose to write in Quechua, highlights one of the great achievements of the Andean peasant, the development of the potato, unknown in Europe till the conquest. The nativo or lengua vaca, the tongue of the cow, is so called because of its shape and its thin, pinkish skin which rubs off easily, revealing a snowy-white flesh more powdery than the commercial variety, the white or 'Irish' potato. There was plenty of time for such comparisons in a long-drawn-out, meditative meal with many finishes which turned out to be merely digestive pauses, after which Faustino waved his heavy hand at us urging us to have one more. I leant forward and turned over a few, thoughtful as a judge, before selecting one I felt was appropriate to that particular stage of my appetite.

'The food of the gods,' I told Faustino, taking oh-just-one more sliver of cheese. And so it seemed, sitting back in the warm dry earth, looking down, way down into the valley to the matchstick bridge over the Santa Eulalia from where the bus had taken a straining hour to climb, and across at the improbable lightning-shaped tracks up mountains which in the late afternoon sun were the dusty blue of a dragonfly's wing.

As we made our way to San Pedro de Casta, Miguel and Abraham pointed out to me the ancient Inca water channels, stone lip leading to stone lip, sunk or cut into the hillside, leading down into the valley. Wherever you go in the Andes you must descend into a valley first. It was still hot and the air thin and everyone else, walking steadily, was catching us up: the girls with their cattle, the small boy with his backful of sticks, using his large machete as a walking-stick. Open-mouthed he stared at us, one finger up his nose, as we overtook him. I heard him whistling behind us, but when we stopped to rest – when I stopped to rest and my companions very courteously waited for me – so did he. There was the same feeling here as in the Colca and Amantani of a medieval tableau, of peasants making their way home from the fields as the sun was sinking.

When we entered the narrow, stone-flagged streets of the village and climbed the wide-spaced steps to the project house, progress was even slower than my breathlessness had dictated. Abraham and Miguel were well respected in the community and already I could see they had complementary qualities which would make them a formidable team. Abraham, in his mid-twenties, had a supple energy and an openness which reminded me of older boys

I had myself been captivated by as a child; qualities which were balanced by the solid dependability of the older Miguel: the rock. For myself, I was introduced as 'un amigo de Ingeniero Mazon,' which guaranteed me a warm reception.

Among one group of well-wishers, one man in a wide straw hat and leather jacket, clearly drunk, wanted to shake hands with me again immediately. We exchanged a few words, then one of them said they had to be going to a funeral and they strode off up a steep alleyway.

At the house I met Enrique Pinto and Miguel Angel, two young musicians who were the mainstays behind the other half of the project. This was to preserve and encourage the folklore traditions of the Andes. With this aim they had welded a group of young children and young men into what they called the Communidad Cultural de Rosa Alarco, named after a famous folklorist who died in 1980. She claimed, 'folklore music is the most authentic and spontaneous expression of the feeling of el pueblo, the village.' There was not much time to go into any of that, though, as Enrique and Miguel Angel were hurrying to give out cane pipes to their band to take part in the aforementioned funeral.

The deceased's house was on the corner of the village square. Mourners were clustered around it when we arrived. We waited; I didn't know for what. Then suddenly the 'cortège' burst from the house, the black coffin lurching in the middle of a crowd of mourners. Behind them, a drum, two oboes, a small tuba and a trumpet thumped out what was to my ears a discordant, brassy tune. As they passed me, on their half-run to the church door, I noted one of the front pallbearers was none other than the leather-jacketed, straw-hatted hand-shaker I had met earlier. The edge of the coffin was knocking his hat over his eyes, threatening a moment of real black comedy before he threw it to someone near at hand.

It was a short stop at the church for a brief blessing, then we were all, the whole pueblo it seemed, funnelling into the path which led up to the cemetery. We followed behind the bobbing black coffin: the women, straw hats pale in the dying light, babies on their backs; the men, whose hats were so old and battered, it was difficult to tell now of what they were made.

The small band of cane pipes, cymbals and drum took over with 'El Condor Pasa'. I had heard it so often in Peru, but now, played slowly with the solemn, weighty refrain of the bass drum, it was strangely fitting.

We entered the walled cemetery and climbed up to its highest level. Here the familial mourners gathered round the one open niche where the coffin was to be interred and cemented up; an Andean, which is most often to say an Inca, funerary tradition. As the cementing took place in candlelight and the keening wife was comforted, the two bands played constantly – 'Tono y responso,' Miguel whispered – and candles were lit before other graves.

From the cemetery I looked down on San Pedro on its spit of land rimmed by the Andes; young upstarts compared to Scotland's ancient crones. They glowed with health now as if lit from within in the dying light: but inside minutes they had turned into high black silhouettes, a ribbon of red above them, like a bench of lords. Such grand beauty was not alone in softening the occasion. The children's music, with its light, breathy pipes and its tinkly cymbals, at times sounded almost jolly.

'No, it's not a sad occasion,' said Miguel. 'It's just a tradition, something the whole village shares in.' And they were there to share, to bear witness, as much as to mourn. In fact at times the situation almost assumed levity. When the brass band were called for, because they had not reached the level of the grave, there were outbreaks of laughter as they pushed their way towards the coffin. As it darkened further, groups of children play-fought on the cemetery's slopes and the girl cooks from Casagayan that afternoon called to me, 'Hola! Tom. Tom. Tom. Hola!' and giggled together.

A donkey brayed. A bell rang. These echoing sounds were the outside world.

Bottles of anisado were passed round and there was the unmistakable splash of a man urinating on the concrete slab of a grave in the darkness: it sounded too needful to be a grudge. The shadow of another man stood momentarily paralysed on a slope, like someone on a tightrope, before reaching the safety of flat land. The drunk pallbearer leant passed me, scratching his head and asking everyone if they had seen his hat.

With the cementing finished, the deceased's nephew made a speech thanking the village for its kindnesses. Then an old friend made a rambling but warm homily, the recurring theme of which was 'Rich or poor, we are all amigos in San Pedro.' During both speeches people turned and made vain shush noises towards the band who were sitting chatting together, amicably passing round the anisado.

After the burial, as I waited with a small group outside the cemetery for the body of the procession, a man handed round cigarettes in a ritual of sharing. On the slow, rough road back into the village the steps of the band were lit by children cupping the flames of candles in their hands.

In the bare house of the dead man we crowded in on benches or pressed against the walls for platefuls of vegetable soup, rice, potatoes and tripe. I had not realised it was the dead man's house we were being ushered into and felt momentarily uncomfortable. Abraham assured me it was not presumptuous of me to be there and there did seem to be a generous acceptance of my presence. I remembered the words of the sympathetic director of Foptur I had spoken to who did not wish to be named. 'You know,' she said, 'this isn't like coming to Europe. There are people here, especially in the mountains, very poor but with big hearts and, speaking personally, I don't think many tourists are a good thing for them. Will Amantani be the same in a few years?' Or, I thought, the close mesh that is San Pedro de Casta?

The next day Eufronio Obispo the cheese-maker, with justifiable pride, underlined my conclusions. 'We are very different in the Andes from in Europe. We feel intensely our relationships within our families and in our community. We are very close.'

I was fortunate to be in San Pedro for the last day of the Fiesta de las Cruces which that night would be celebrated by music and dancing from eleven till three in the morning.

Enrique tapped my shoulder as I lay drowsing in my bunk, and we walked out into the chill night. He had been coming here for many years before the project began paying him to teach the children. If I had not known he came out from Lima each weekend I could have painted him as the Wandering Minstrel strolling up a dusty track, a bag of pipes over his shoulder, a thumb-shaped hat on his head.

In the uneven square at the top of the village, he shielded the faint light coming from the community hall and pointed out to me the four stars known as Las Cruces. 'It's called a Christian festival, but you ask why it's held at this time of the year. Well, it's because now is the time when the constellation of Las Cruces is at its height.

Many festivals in the Andes are much older than when Christianity was imposed; but Christianity made use of them.'

The most important fiesta in San Pedro de Casta was La Fiesta del Agua. 'It's held in October,' Enrique told me. 'The fiesta is concerned with clearing the channels from the lakes which silt up. The water is stopped off and the channels cleared. But it's both a physical cleaning and a magical cleaning. Each day of work – it takes a week – is accompanied by song and dancing.'

To Rosa Alarco who made an extensive study of the Fiesta del Agua in San Pedro, 'The rite symbolises the loving relationship – relación amorosa – between man and the natural elements,' a feeling that is very strong in the Andes. Eufronio Obispo for example told me that each thunder had a different name depending on which direction it came from. 'We think they are all brothers, playing or quarrelling.' A Quechua saying, stuck up on the wall of our room where I had also found articles on Rosa Alarco, captured this feeling as it affected the earth. 'El hombre es tierra que anda. Somos tierra que anda. Hombres – tierra.' (Man is earth that walks. We are earth that walks. Man – earth.)

Inside the community hall six brightly dressed girl dancers called Chuncha representing people of the forest were executing a ritual dance accompanied by a cane pipe and a harp. One of them was a plucky boy in drag which added to the strangeness of the event. In the Incas' time, Miguel told me, the forest and the mountains were not such separate realities as now. The dancers' movements and the music were jerky, formal, hypnotic. 'They use European instruments,' Rosa Alarco wrote, 'but their pentatonic scale prevails; they imitate the choreography of the minuet and the quadrille, but they conserve the vigorous rhythm of their ancestors.' A genuine mestizo musical form.

This evening, however, ritual was short-lived. The prevailing atmosphere was of a Highland ceilidh with an Andean accent. The smallest boys in the cane group stood on benches, their bodies jerking with each blow, their sandalled feet tapping, as Enrique, Miguel Angel and Abraham drove them on with a physical energy which built and built into a frantic hothouse rhythm.

Small, generous women moved along the seated company with a glass and a bottle of anisado. I had a few vigorous dances, mostly with a woman with few teeth, who stared straight ahead at my chest and with a whimsical smile guided me one way then the other at will, and when we were in a reel pulled me about with her strong, short arms as violently as she could. She was plainly a distant sister to the "Wife in High Spirits", who MacDiarmid had encountered in a pub in Edinburgh's High Street: 'The heich skeich auld cat was fair in her element/Wanton as a whirlwind.'

There was much dust kicked up and many strong handshakes and invitations to houses whenever I wanted, 'because this is my village and you're welcome.' The schoolteacher was pointed out to me, sitting alone in a drunken gloom.

The next morning in Eufronio's house (earthy potato bunkers – the smell of the Peruvian highlands), we breakfasted on boiled potatoes, cheese and hot milk and oats. There was an easy generosity to Eufronio's hospitality, a dignity which was stolen from or lost by many who went down to the coast.

Miguel and I were going to climb up to Marcahuasi, a combination of Inca ruins and distinctive stone formations on a volcanic plateau high above San Pedro. 'Eat well,' Miguel advised me, 'because there's nothing till four o'clock this afternoon.'

It was a steep climb in dry, searing heat. Miguel, with a tolerant big-heartedness, coaxed me on during moments of breathlessness and doubt, stopping at any point on the twisting path at which we might justify a rest. It was, though, 'vale la pena.' We watched a condor slowly, majestically circling higher and higher and felt ourselves from Marcahuasi sharing a condor's eye-view of the valley. We held it, San Pedro and the road that so tortuously winds through and up to such heights, within one gasping glance.

The Incas who lived here, who regarded all irregularities in nature as sacred, must have held these colossal, cliffsided boulders with a special reverence. 'The Man', 'The Turtle' – each one was named with a name that I assume had lasted, as so much else had, from a time way before the extensive sheep-pen of ruins which covered the hill-top was a thriving community. But the awesome qualities of height, space, mass and time were matched by the delicacy of the mountain flowers: bright swathes of orange and yellow; small discoveries of delicate pinks and blues. Miguel gave me all this.

And the whole weekend we ate in houses where the reception was warm, where smiles came readily and money was never to be mentioned. But when the bus from Chosica entered Lima proper, everyone seemed cowed, that openness once more held in check. Lima was too various: it assaulted the senses with its anomalies, its grime, its greyness, its dull, sad stalls; the pressure of living. The back of a book of poems by Cesar Vallejo I had picked up had praised him for capturing, 'A manner of seeing the world that characterises the Peruvian man of the Andes: Una viviencia del dolor, con una angustia por un más allá desconocido.' (A life of pain with an anguished desire for an unknown world.) It seemed to me at that moment that words like *dolor* and *angustia* were far more applicable to the life of the poor Limeño.

> Little star of heaven
> Lend me your brightness,
> For the life of this world
> Is a dark night.
>
> *Quechua.*

'Ciao,' said Enrique and was gone. Then, with a smile, Abraham.

Miguel and I shared a taxi; he battering the taxi fare far lower than I ever could, or needed to. He thanked me effusively for my address; we embraced and said goodbye.

I think now perhaps it was Miguel, with his soft man-boy's face, his thin moustache and accommodating silences, who walked off on his splayed feet with the last of my bitterness. I recognised him as one with David Ricalde, with Abraham, Enrique and Miguel Angel: young people with optimism, energy and integrity, who did not want Peru to be a European country or fit any other kind of theoretical straitjacket, but wanted it only to become what(ever) it truly was.

'This Crazy Country'
LIMA, ADIOS!

At the Colegio de San Silvestre I take one of Alan's classes for a writing session. 'How about this, Alan? Imagine you are one of the beggars. Write a poem about . . .'

'Don't mention the poor!' he instructs me.

The headmistress has just gone into hiding with her husband who's had a death-threat from MRTA because of some business arrangement he's made. Behind the high fence and the guards, all seems remarkably calm. Alan fetches me tea and biscuits and there are tittering smiles in the corridor for the blond male PE teacher. One girl writes, 'I'd like to live in New Zealand where there is no violence or poverty . . .'

Then to lunch with Antonio in Miraflores's Café Haiti. My treat. He is keeping South American time; he's an unruffled hour late. He's having trouble with his editor, an affair superficially concerned with politics; but Antonio thinks there is a deeper personality clash. It may mean him giving up his job which counts for two-thirds of his salary. Moreover he considers himself to be far more of a journalist than a teacher – it's how he has lived for the past twenty years. He is chainsmoking, wild-eyed.

'You know,' he tells me, 'for you, you're lucky to be here at this precise moment in history. For you know, this is a very definite turning point, not for places like San Pedro de Casta, but for the cities yes.'

That is the intellectual's view. The husband and father cannot be so objective. 'This bloody country! I don't want us to be rich. I don't want us to be West Germany. I just want us to be as we were ten years ago, that's all.'

The times are crushing Antonio's spirit. He remembers better ones. 'Ah, it was wonderful to be Latin American in Swinging

168

London. For the girls! You could say, "I am the son of the owner of a huge hacienda," to one; or, "I am the son of a poor peasant, working on a huge hacienda," depending on the girl.' With his laughter, a ghostly boyishness returns.

Poor sleep. A case of nerves about Huancayo – Sendero territory. At Desamparados in the early morning I look around for sweets to combat altitude sickness as the notice advises: 'Keep with you suckers for eating during the route.' But I am told the line is damaged and the train not running.

A taxi driver tells me it's just as well, that it's a very dangerous area now. Mark had told me nonchalantly, 'You should go to the monastery there. It's just near where these sixty-two guys were shot a couple of weeks back.' Cheers.

The morning after my disappointment at not getting to ride Jim Leigh's toy train to Huancayo, I read that the previous day Sendero Luminoso decreed a seventy-two-hour strike in the centre of the country: namely in the departments of Junin, Cerro de Pasco and Huanuco. They dynamited the Banco de los Andes, the Mercado Mayorista, the Central Hidroelectrica in the district of Tambo and a hospital under the auspices of the Guardia Civil. In Huancayo itself, between the evening and the morning of 9 May, there were thirty explosions.

I also read that fourteen kilometres from La Merced, a bus was stopped by fifty Senderistas in the early morning. After everyone showed identification, two members of the Fuerza Aerea del Peru were taken out and shot.

The report on page seventeen of *El Comercio* with the quaint, Lima-centric heading 'Trouble with the line', states that there is a heavy military presence, but an atmosphere of fear among the population. Everything is shut. The headlines in *Expreso* are more direct: 'Terror Reina en Huancayo' and 'Por Temor: Huanuco Paralizado'.

How wrong I was! San Pedro de Casta teeters on the edge of a world full of 'dolor' and 'angustia'. The five million who live in ramshackle housing in 'Greater Lima' are testament to that fact.

Time on my hands. I take a taxi to Rimac with a plump, middle-aged taxi driver – usually they're young and lean – who makes the front of his Beetle feel like a cramped cockpit, and who is actually proud of his city: he just thinks it's a little overcrowded. 'Fifty years ago in Lima, there were four hundred thousand people; now eight million. It's too many.'

We drive through the pink-walled streets, past the faded bloom of Rimac: the Plaza de Toros, the Alameda park – Old Lima, now designated a national monument. Los pueblos jovenes, the shanty-towns where displaced campesinos become the urban poor, rise up steeply at its very edge, looking as if they're made out of dust.

'With a little bit of money spent on it . . .' I start, but he turns to me with a hurt little frown. Why dent this lone enthusiast? To please him I walk down Alameda, the elegant parque de paseo of the aristocracy, as he leans on his car in the heat.

'At night, though, when it's all lit up, it's *muy* bonita – preciosa.'

A night walk through leafy San Isidro, beneath the scent of eucalyptus, extravagant bougainvillea. During the day key intersections in these areas are staffed by money-changers – cambistas – who run alongside cars or throw themselves perilously in front of them. In the cocaine season, when I arrived, it was snowing dollars. Today a dollar changes hands for 2,900 intis compared to 1,200 three months ago. There's an unsavoury machismo amongst gringos about scoring the most favourable exchange rate.

To the rich (mostly all blancos), the mark of class here, as in California, is the quality of your protection; the control you exercise over your environment. Pretty villas and ersatz haciendas with gardens in bloom, sprinklers on the lawns, are seen through tripartite spiked fences. With the soft whine of an automatic door, a giant, four-wheel drive Toyota slips on to the street. The outside world comes with the eerie squeals of the ice-cream sellers on their tricycles, blowing their hooters, a plaintive, maddening sound, or in the occasional shouts of '¡Platanos baratos!' '¡Flores! ¡Flores!' from wandering pedlars. At night dobermans bark and snarl when you pass; security men kill time and laugh together at street corners.

In a bakery in San Isidro, half a dozen croissants cost more than a policeman earns in a day. This is Lima, European Lima; the rest just an appendage that's slowly sinking into grime, into history. The big irony, though, is that Europe doesn't care about any part of it any more.

I meet two teachers from Alan's school in a restaurant in San Isidro: two jolly escapees from comprehensives in the north of

England. They tell me a bomb went off last week two hundred
metres from where they live. But they're not going to move till
the embassy starts pulling people out. 'Well, that bomb was only
two hundred metres away and that didn't make us think about
moving, did it? And let's face it, any nearer and we wouldn't have
to bother!' Mr and Mrs Jack Spratt look at each other and laugh with
excitement. Their eyes glow at mention of the state of emergency
Lima has been under for months now; positively shine at the widely
held view that after Beirut it's the second most dangerous city in the
world.

President Alan Garcia, as effective with terrorists as he is with
the economy, is trying to instil the bulldog spirit into the shocked
and terrified inhabitants of Huancayo whom he has criticised for
succumbing to the terror. He exhorts them 'to lose their fear and
make a united front against subversion'.

The Church, in the form of La Asamblea General de la Con-
ferencia Episcopal Peruana, in a document entitled 'Peru, Choose
Life!' declares that the actual socio-economic and political crisis is a
moral crisis and until there is a 'general moral conversion', there will
be no beating the crisis. To whom, I wonder, is *this* addressed?

Tomorrow I fly north to Iquitos, Peru's jungle capital.

Alan and I take a taxi down to Rosa Nautica, a bar and restaurant
confection on Lima's seafront. A wooden walkway, lined by souvenir
shops, reaches out to the circular rooms. You can take a bicycle cart
the length of it, driven by a youth dressed like a bell-boy. Inside we
sit at a table with a porthole at its centre, surrounded by geraniums
and ferns, beneath slowly revolving propellors. Outside, the grey,
oleaginous sea ('And the Pacific wasn't terrific . . .') shushes against
the supports.

Alan tells me the really rich don't come here any more. Uniquely
among shoreside restaurants, Rosa Nautica has refused to pay
protection money to Sendero. Thus, on the way in and out, you
must pass six soldiers with machine-guns, a paddy-wagon, an
elegant white pillbox with trained machine-gun, and an eagerly
growling doberman.

In the middle of the night I go to the toilet. There is no electricity.
Later I am woken by Alan pouring bottles of water into the cistern.
The apartment has a faint smell of rotten eggs. 'You're told to keep

water,' he sighs, 'but the water goes off, that's the trouble.'

Mark has told me of the rumour that Sendero will try to shut down the city as a show of strength on their anniversary. 'This is how it's going to end,' says Alan, a dark, shuffling shadow with two huge plastic Coke bottles in his hands, 'nothing exciting or dramatic, just nasty, fetid and messy.'

I am reminded that *The Real Life of Alejandro Mayta* doesn't end with the imagined apocalypse either, but with the duller reality of 'the garbage that's invading every neighbourhood in the capital of Peru'. I too have a fictional ending to my time in Lima. It includes a searching interview with Vargas Llosa, and a mistimed but shattering trip into the heart of darkness, Sendero-locked Huancayo, to confront my fears. However I have to say the truer experience, for me, is this: not (yet) 'nasty, fetid and messy', but inconclusive . . . frayed . . .

'*¿Qué te parece Lima?*'

I do the last photocopying of all my extant writings at the British Council (once burnt and all that!) and go to meet Toni for lunch.

The two biggest sellers on the street corners of Miraflores are red roses by the bucketful (I keep walking and a dozen are thrust upon me for the original price of one), and editions of *Time* magazine with a short article titled 'Caught in a Fatal Spin Towards Turmoil'; sub-headed 'Can a country cope with terrorism, stifling poverty, oppressive foreign debt and 10,000% inflation?' A nod of interest from the outside world.

Toni confesses she is '*irrationally* fond of Peru'. I'm put in mind of phone calls to the few Latin American vets I was in touch with before I left Scotland. Their voices yearned as they described the places I should visit, children crying in the background. There's the tantalising, disturbing line at the end of Michael Herr's *Dispatches*: 'Perhaps Vietnam was the happy childhoods we never had.'

Friends who know something of the situation in Peru have written to Toni, almost demanding to know how she can keep her children in such danger, especially since Sendero have recently murdered foreign aid workers in Apurimac and Huancayo. It is not an issue for her yet. 'And what,' she argues, 'would I do as a single mother in Britain? This is far from perfect, but I have a good job, a maid to help me and the kids are in good schools.' And, of course, she is never bored here.

Alan is delivering the children to Toni's after school when I am hailing a taxi. I leave him, unshaven, his eyes full of anxieties, holding tightly on to his children's hands on the edge of the pavement on Avenida Larco.

Taxi to the airport. This taxi driver has been working in Brooklyn and will go back there in July. He is one of the fifty per cent of the population who reputedly want to leave Peru. For the others there is a car sticker which reads, 'Esta es mi patria y de aquí no me voy.' (This is my country and I'm not leaving.)

'There is no future for my children here,' he states bluntly. At the moment he does two jobs, driving taxis and working for a security firm, to survive. Which is one reason why Lima's taxi drivers are such an informed body to talk to – though they may not always know where you want to go. Each trip begins with a bargaining, followed by, 'Hey, watch my door', which is usually hanging on one hinge. 'Times are hard in Peru,' they tell you; to which I reply, 'I know. I have been robbed twice.' They shake their heads at this or nod towards scrawny kids with rags in their hands who pounce on the windscreen at traffic lights on the pitted road out: 'This crazy country,' they say or, as my last taxi driver in Lima says, 'Our country,' turning his thumbs down, 'our country is really going down . . .'

Three Men in a Boat
IQUITOS

In a dilapidated wooden bar with a veranda overhanging the tips of river boats. Beyond them, I'm staring into dark space. The Amazon. It's a ticklish feeling, like the first time beneath palm trees in the Sahara.

It's a strange bar, harshly lit. In one part an unshaven man with a grey skin and a large belly watches TV from a hammock, his bum brushing the floor. Two small girls wrestle on a bed beside him. A pregnant woman in a soiled slip, her face puffed with drink, walks around aimlessly and is fed glasses of beer by a local tour guide. Tomorrow he is going up the jungle for eight days. 'But the *real* jungle,' he insists. He tells me Iquitos is being discriminated against. 'We have the *jungle*, but Foptur won't advertise us; just Cuzco, Cuzco, Cuzco.' He tells me how safe it is here; no robbers, no terrorism – calm, tranquilo.

Mid-morning. I go down to 'the port', an eccentric-looking bunch of river boats jostling beside rickety pontoons, and ask about a boat to Islandia at the borders of Colombia and Brazil. From there (a journey of two or three days), I'll catch another boat to Manaus – 'the Capital of the Amazonias'.

The chalkboard reads, '*Yurimaguas*: Lunes 5p.m.' There is no need to buy a ticket till Monday itself. A fat man in a vest spits out this information at me as he spits out the coating of a nut he's eating. I look at him, his sweat patches, and at the wooden boat – the *African Queen* and its captain, both gone to seed.

Iquitos seethes with a frontier life. Oil exploration, not rubber, is evidently what fuels it now. From the market I look across to Belen, the shanty river town clustered fifty yards away where some of Herzog's *Fitzcarraldo* was shot. Beyond Belen: the brown width of the Amazon, the bright green islands, the slivers of black canoes.

174

It's difficult to connect this jungle island with Lima, with San Pedro de Casta – 'the three realities'.

'What I like to do,' Barry had told me, 'is grab a six-pack and just ride around for hours in one of these scooter-powered rickshaws they've got. See all the decrepit mansions the rubber barons built last century.' But I'm chock-a-block with Peru. I want to be gone *now* However I've just met Freddie, who seems to hang about the open-air café on a corner of Plaza de Armas as much as I do. He's dark, squat and powerful-looking, as if some great weight had been dropped on him, flattened his head and bent his legs, but he hadn't broken. 'I'm Freddie. You've read the *Handbook*?' and he nods, before I answer, 'Ah, yes, so you're Freddie.'

'Freddie organises survival courses in the jungle,' the *Handbook* reads, 'and you learn to build your own camp, find your own food etc. Be warned, however: he has to approve of you and your level of fitness and stamina, not you of him.'

Freddie shakes his head and spits like a water-snake at my mention of the *Yurimaguas* leaving on Monday. 'But it says it on the chalk . . .' I start.

With the help of the *Handbook*, I find my way to a recommended restaurant through the warm, dimly lit streets, catching glimpses through open doors and windows of people rocking before a TV, their walls alive with garish religious icons. Feeling easy, I catch a sudden nostalgia for the Dominican Republic.

The restaurant, a rickle of wicker tables and chairs behind a wicker screen, is empty; but a family of women – granny, mother and daughter – gather round me, smiling with great amusement. Granny sits beside me peering up into my face as she tells me all the food here comes from the forest. Menus are banded about to great effect, but it's *paiche* again, the meaty river fish which grows to lengths of two metres.

Granny tells me as I eat that it's dangerous to walk around here after dark. 'We have terrorists here and they kill people.'

'But I have been told there are no problems here . . .'

'It is the people who live here who know. I'm telling you, as a friend, be back at your hotel at nine; no later than ten . . .'

'Calm! Tranquil! Pah!' says Freddie. 'More drugs pass through here than anywhere.' Whatever, Freddie is right about one thing –

the *Yurimaguas* isn't leaving. The *Maria Elena* is, though there is much doubt. Still, I buy a hammock in hope. Iquitos would seem to be the perfect place from which to leave Peru. An air of doubt hangs over everything like the black vultures over the waste of Belen. Sense impressions cluster – putrid smells: dog shit, human shit; a naked man hugging himself; a crying woman, near naked, crouching in a shop-front; 'Dolares! Dolares!' and the Irish green of the islands.

Esben is young, friendly and confident; blond and blue-eyed like a Danish pop-singer. We will go together, watch each other's gear, be friends. He has the confidence of having worked in Brazil for the past two years for Scandinavian Airlines and not being afraid to seek help. 'That airport in Lima, you know it. I was so scared and I got into this taxi and it was all rusted. I shouted to the driver, "Stop, I want to get out. I want to get out!" In the end I asked a policeman to come and ride with me into Lima.'

'And he did it?' He did it. Esben has that kind of immediate charm. I note too that when he talks to South American men, he punches them very lightly on the shoulder or brushes their forearms with his hand. 'It's the Brazilian way,' he tells me. It must work for, somehow or other, he also got a soldier to ride with him on the local train to Machu Picchu. I'll stick with him.

Freddie, slumped in his chair, a cross between a sumo wrestler and an upturned tortoise, tells us for certain the *Maria Elena* isn't leaving. He is willing to bet us twenty dollars. But we have been down to the harbour we tell him. Esben has even asked the captain, '¿Seguro que sí?'

'Seguro sin falta,' the captain replied. Freddie shakes his head and does a couple of dry spits.

We go down to the boat, the size of a small pleasure steamer, and tie up our hammocks next to a French couple who have been trying to get out of here for days. We swing with confidence. I leave the boat to buy a couple of Cokes; come back to see people leaving down the slippery planks. Must be 'All ashore, who's going ashore' time I think. But Esben waits for me with his folded hammock. Amazing Peru. Amazing at *being* Peru: and so meekly everyone accepts it.

Today at the port they are sure. Today there is no doubt. *Expreso* carries the jaunty headline 'Janero – Adiós el Inti', and last night's annoyance at the *Maria Elena* has been tempered by reality i.e. we will hold no spite against her – we just want to be on a boat that's sure to be leaving!

According to Freddie, who now holds court in the café, wearing the pompous rectitude of royalty, there are three possibles: the *Maria Elena*, the *Yurimaguas* and the *Santa Barbara*. Last night the *Maria Elena* didn't go because she lacked passengers. Tonight they will sit and keep everyone guessing till one's belly is satisfied. Freddie advises against the *Santa Barbara*. It's all tin and the journey would be like going into an oven for three days. Thank you, Freddie. I can now believe that people on your trips do cry, tell you they hate you and wish you dead. If I was weak, hungry and mosquito-bitten, trying to spear a *paiche* with your self-satisfied cat-grin on me, I could easily wish you transposed. Once it's all over, you say they love you. Got to take your word for that one.

We go down about four. Fruit sellers have moved on to the dusty square where earlier wiry, glistening men with bare feet played a fire-cracker game of concentrated football.

With our bags we edge carefully down the muddy slope, parts of which are already smooth and treacherous. It smells of rotting, decomposing vegetation. We rest a hand on the pillars of the pier to help us down. A location scout for some *film noir* would pick this as the place-where-the-body-was-found. I imagine its dark corners lit up by arc lights, detectives on the scene.

We must cross two slippery planks and the oily, metal floor of the *Juliana*, the boat which featured in *Fitzcarraldo*, to board the *Maria Elena*, nuzzling its blunt head between the *Juliana* and the *Yurimaguas*. The last at least has definitely opted out of the leaving stakes. 'Mañana', the chalk reads – whatever that means.

There are a few hammocks up already: people waiting in a Latin time-means-nothing-adjusted way. And matching their lethargy is Alex; at eighteen a natural South American traveller, here to wash off a Winchester school education. 'I just wanted to go somewhere no one I knew had been.' With plimsoles he daren't take off and threadbare jeans, dangling a leg over his hammock and occasionally clearing a curled wing of hair from his face, he has a beatific smile for the whole continent's vast uncertainties.

The lower deck fills up with sacks and drums. When I leave to buy some bananas I pass men bent beneath their loads, their firm bodies covered with sweat and streaked with oil. One insists on shaking my hand. 'Give me a dollar for something to eat.' His eyes aren't friendly. Of course they're not.

The hammocks run into each other now. When I look along the deck there's an abstract of texture and colour: it's too dense to really swing. So many hammocks can't be wrong! The engine runs and runs, a tractor sound, and the decks fill with fumes. It's after seven: it's eight, we're leaving now. It's now after nine. But they've taken names and money – it's looking good. Let's hope so, for we've seen a full *Santa Barbara* reverse and steam off. 'Islandia. Hoy', it said. And the others move off south to Yurimaguas, to Pucalpa. Jungle towns – dank, humid, greenly living.

We talk. Alex has been robbed four times and had to replace all his camera equipment. He gives me my favourite robbery story. When he was swimming in Pisco, the friends he was travelling with took all his clothes, leaving only his hat on the beach. An old Peruvian walking along the beach saw the hat, liked the look of it, tried it for size and swopped it for his own. I see the scene performed by Chaplin or Keaton.

We talk. Esben is in love with a tour guide he met in Lima, not with the schoolgirl I saw him with a day later in Iquitos. He doesn't speak Spanish, only Portuguese, but they get by. Alex is in love with a girl he met in Santiago in Chile. He doesn't speak Spanish, nor she English but it is special he thinks. 'Go for it!' they tell each other.

We talk; and then someone says, surprised, 'We're moving!' And we are, gliding back from between the two larger ships into the black waters of the Amazon. Now we've curved round and, in spite of the engine, move almost silently downriver beside the lights of Iquitos which shine in broad ribbons on the black waters of the Amazon.

Of the Amazon. For this is it: you're actually *on* the Amazon. I'm remembering one time, years ago, a French container ship docked at Glencaple on the River Nith. It was such an exotic occasion, the newspaper carried a double-page photograph of it:

> Then one night, after a few drinks,
> three of us left the rooted crowd,
> picked our way through the black, brooding
> graveyard of overnight containers –
> and boarded. The insistent throb

of disco was a sounding-board
for silence – insectlike, complete –
as we felt our way to the prow
like smugglers. There we took command.
The river brought us the faint tang

of the sea and endless shots of night
within which we lost the landscape's
bearings. Mountain, forest, hillsides –
all dissolved in darkness. Lights
sparkled here and there along the river's edge –

the friendly lights of settlements
where succour would be given to each
who had a need. So this – this
was Nile, Amazon, Limpopo . . .
Linking arms, we made a pact

to dissolve what we'd become, to hold
on to this profligate world
of dreams and possibilities,
as the dull clang of living history
sounded hard beneath our feet.

Freddie told us how an anaconda once rose out of the water behind
one of his tour group: he had to shoot it first time. 'You think you
see the real Amazon,' he scoffed. 'Not true.' And now, when we
move out still further into its centre current and are drifting down
the real black river, past the dark breath of the trees lining the bank,
I realise 'the Amazon', like the Nile and the Limpopo, is elsewhere
and for ever out of reach . . .

Travel. I think of Neruda's poem comparing writing poems to
ironing: smoothing out the creases. The poems I like best give a
kind of release, a sense of completion:

I'll just stretch out on the wet sand, shoeless,
close my eyes, & shut my heart
like the saltwater snails,
the hard red ones.

Travel cannot offer such an experience. The intensity required to be
of this place – however fleetingly – the energy to respond, to attempt
to understand, dissipates. The other life and the other self beckon:

B becomes a blur.

> *So you never did see the bar-tailed lark,*
> *the bar-tailed lark, the bar-tailed lark,*
> *so you never did see the bar-tailed lark?*
> "No, mate, I never did."

This trip must be the closest return to infancy possible – rocking and sleeping in the heat, eating (chicken and rice, chicken and rice, chicken and rice) and sucking on a cool beer, as we watch the green world drift by. Groups of men in vests crowd a few pairs of hammocks, playing cards as their wives look after the children; but our somnambulant routine is only broken when we bend our heads to go downstairs to fetch another beer or to use the toilet whose pipe shows the brown waters of the river.

I'm struggling through *Plant and the Planet* by Anthony Huxley which I've carted round with me all this time. If I don't read it now . . .

'Hey, get this,' I enthuse, '"Solomon Islanders claim to be able to kill trees . . . by creeping up on them before dawn and suddenly uttering piercing yells close to the trunk. After a month the tree is said to die as a result of shock from such frequent and violent awakenings."' Esben and Alex nod tolerantly, swop tapes for their Walkmans, tap out the beat on their thighs.

At darkness the plastic covers are brought down – and when it rains. The crew sense the squally wind warning and always unwrap the sheeting on time. We listen to the rain beat on the plastic.

My hammock is string and therefore cold. (Teach you, cheapskate!) I'm awake for the grey dawn, the mist on the river. *Look! We have come through.* To breakfast on hot milk mixed with oats, and rolls spread with margarine from a huge tin box.

Renata, a grinding German-Australian, sleeps next to Esben. She scowls at him when he wakes: 'All night, moving around like a little boy . . .' She is dressed half South American vet and half SAS. When Esben shows us his packets of snaps from his trip so far, mostly bleached scenes of Esben on a beach with his arms around some handsome young men or girls, she tuts over his shoulder. For some reason she will not tell us how long she's been travelling, financing herself it would seem by sending home local goods: forty twine bags from Iquitos, twenty sweaters from Puno . . .

I think we're meant to think she's done everything and we nothing.
But frankly, none of us could care about all the names with which she
badges herself; not when there are blue dolphins around and herons
and egrets like candleflames . . .

We sit out of our hammocks for each village; a scatter of stilted huts,
often with a football pitch of red mud at the water's edge. The boat is
an event. At every small stop a cluster of villagers comes to watch.
Sometimes canoes paddle out to pass on bananas and papayas. At
such stops, while Esben smiles and collects 'clicks' from the girls,
Alex is given to surges of photographic energy. He is going to Oxford
first, but really wants to be a film director. This afternoon he hauls
himself and his camera up on to the roof of the boat, jeans down at
his hips, stomach like a wash-board. Yesterday, for his amusement,
I read him my collection of Camera Stories which I have just closed
with this peach of the genre from a traveller in Iquitos: 'We were just
arriving in Peru; we'd been going about half an hour and there was a
big commotion up ahead. I got the camera out, thinking there's got
to be a picture here somewhere! And as it happened, as we went by,
it was an overturned bus with dead bodies everywhere. I got two
great shots.' What was it Susan Sontag said? 'Life is a movie: death
is a photograph.' And travel?

A sunset fans up from behind the jungle over the still waters: they
seem to seep into the forest itself as to a waterfall's edge. We move
past islands when the rich vegetation is close to us, then into the
broad body of the river again. And the moon comes up like a huge
gold plate, casting a gold arm across the black waters. And black too,
like a cut-out silhouette, the trees of the rainforest – a frieze of hearts,
lungs, arteries; stretching, stretching . . .

And drifting with Esben, with his always-enthusiasm – 'Let's have
a good cake, a nice beer' – and Alex, swinging over his gathering mess
of picnic detritus and camera gear: the perfect young companions.
Three men in a boat. Renata has drifted from us, finding a tame macaw
with clipped wings and a head for numbers preferable company.

At customs we are forced to climb down a slippery, narrow plank
and over deep mud to a small, raised wooden hut. My shoes are
caked with mud when I get there. The others, smarter than me,

leave their shoes on board. But the custom's official refuses to allow them into his office without shoes. We look at each other, aghast. It is another example of deliberate difficulty. Eventually I am stamped by candlelight in the bare office. The others must wait until he deigns to bring the stamp out.

We clamber back up the plank and on to the *Maria Elena*. Peru, even in the middle of the rainforest, at its furthest possible edge, is Peru to the bitter end . . .

> She dreams of a horse
> as melancholy as her name.
> She is called Rosaura
> and she journeys without a hat
> beneath rain which surrounds her
> like the dust of a city
> in ruins. And she dreams
> of a horse which smiles
> in a melancholy way, while the rain
> grows over her head:
> the fine dust of a universe in ruins.
> No one saves her from her dream
> of horses and melancholy,
> so she keeps going beneath the rain,
> with a sad smile
> and doesn't venture
> to lift a hand nor to die
> among the wet ruins.
> From where does this woman come?
> From what tears
> more numerous than the rain
> she has stirred up with its horse and its melancholy?
> She is called Rosaura
> and she journeys without hat or hope
> and leaves only
> a very slight shadow
> over the damp earth.
>
> Rosaura Bajo La Lluvia
> *Rosaura Beneath the Rain*
>
> *Washington Delgado*

Postscript in Rio

I decided to take a final, ruminative walk along Flamengo beach before packing and ordering a taxi for the airport. I was feeling remarkably pleased with myself, having managed to change my flight date with Air France to allow me to watch Flamengo against Fluminense at the fire-cracking Maracana Stadium the night before.

It was a late afternoon in May which was the beginning of autumn in Rio. At the end of the fabulous bay, Sugar Loaf was turning faintly blue, and people on the beach or heading there were scarce.

I was halfway over a pedestrian bridge when a jogger stopped beside me and asked me the time. I showed him my watch. 'Tres y media,' I said as he seemed to have difficulty reading the face. He was in his mid-twenties, black, stripped to the waist with red shorts and a tattoo of some sort on his upper arm. He smiled and I repeated, 'Tres y media.' Then there was a clutch of arms around me and a serrated kitchen knife was at my throat, nicking my hand as it automatically went to protect myself.

'Tranquilo, eh,' a voice breathed in my ear. 'No hay problema.' And there was a slap as Simone de Beauvoir's A *Woman Destroyed* from my back pocket hit the deck. (It had been irritating me too.)

There were four of them running down all these Rohan zips. I felt strangely calm knowing I had nothing on me I would fight for. I sensed their fear, their desperation to be away. I knew instinctively their reluctance to have to hurt me, and they must have known my reluctance to be hurt. The quicker the better for us all.

I held out my wrist and helped one man take my watch off; in his fluster the buckle had seemed to defeat him. They undid my belt and unzipped my trousers looking for the money belt which was in the safety deposit box back at my hotel. Then they were off. Running like mad. I saw the red of my small flip-top notebook in one of their hands. "Hey, Señor! Señor!" I wanted to say the notebook was worthless but I did not have the Portuguese. He

183

looked round all the same and I latched onto the fear in his eyes.

I tidied myself and put my hands in each pocket to feel the insubstantial lack of some cruzados, a wadge of toilet paper and the notebook which had contained a few pressed flowers from Amantani, a bright, petrol-blue butterfly from the spectacular Falls of Iguacu, a note of the exact colouring of Jim Birback's eyes and a badge for South American travellers that Alex and I had designed. Its crest bore the Latin motto: Nihil Pessimi – None of the Worst.

I turned three hundred and sixty degrees twice, each time taking a step back to the hotel; then thought, what's the point? And suddenly I was laughing, a laugh that was coming from a place deep inside me, deeper than . . . *la-de-da,* richer than . . . *la-de-da*: the laugh of someone who has been told a long, obscure joke and just got the punchline.

I twirled round and continued my walk.